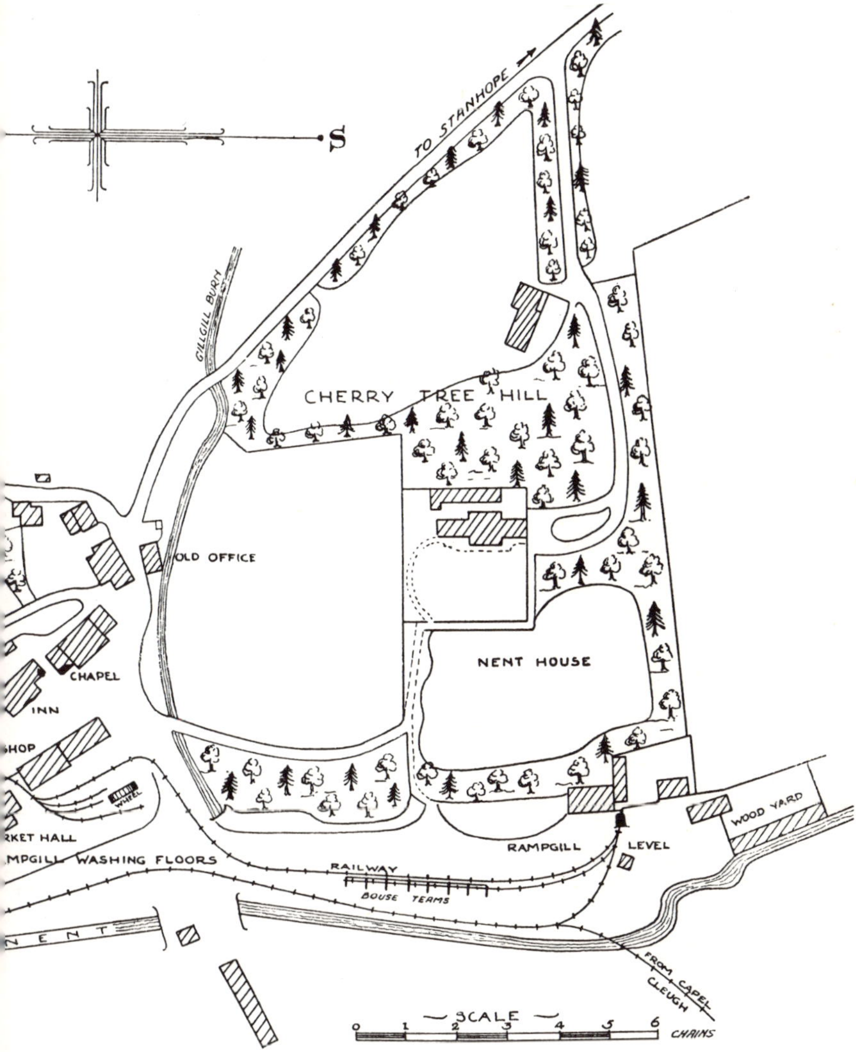
S
TO STANHOPE
GILLGILL BURN
CHERRY TREE HILL
OLD OFFICE
CHAPEL
INN
HOP
WHEEL
RKET HALL
MPGILL WASHING FLOORS
NENT HOUSE
RAILWAY
BOUSE TEAMS
RAMPGILL
LEVEL
WOOD YARD
NENT
FROM CAPEL CLEUGH
SCALE
0 1 2 3 4 5 6
CHAINS

TWO CENTURIES OF INDUSTRIAL WELFARE

The London (Quaker) Lead Company, 1692-1905

The "Office Gate" at Nent House.

TWO CENTURIES OF INDUSTRIAL WELFARE:

The London (Quaker) Lead Company
1692-1905

The Social Policy and Work of the "Governor and Company for Smelting down Lead with Pit Coal and Sea Coal", mainly in Alston Moor and the Pennines

BY

ARTHUR RAISTRICK

KELSALL & DAVIS
1988

First edition 1938
Revised second edition 1977
Republished (with additional photographs) 1988
by

George Kelsall   &   Davis Books Ltd
22, Church Street   140, Westgate Road
Littleborough   Newcastle upon Tyne
Lancashire

ISBN 0 946571 13 9 Kelsall
ISBN 0 946865 08 6 Davis

The publishers of this edition record their thanks to Moorland Publishing Company for allowing their edition to be used for reproduction.

© Arthur Raistrick 1988

Printed and Bound by
SMITH SETTLE
Ilkley Road, Otley
West Yorkshire

CONTENTS

		page
Preface to 1988 Edition		7
Introduction		9
Chapter I		17
Chapter II	Miners' Health	40
Chapter III	Education	56
Chapter IV	Transport	77
Chapter V	Social Policy	94
Chapter VI	Technical Developments	133
Chapter VII	Biographical Notes	146
Index		166

MAPS

1	Nent Head in 1825	Endpapers
2	The London Lead Company's mines	6
3	Roads built by the London Lead Company	121
4	Principal mining leases in North of England	122

PLATES

frontis	The "Office Gate" at Nent House	
I	Nenthead House	33
II	The Killhope Waterwheel, Weardale	33
III	Nent Head Smelt Mill	34
IV	Nent Head and Rampgill dressing floors	34
V	The Assay House at Nent Head	67
VI	Cornish stamps at Nent Head	67
VII	The Garrigill Road	68
VIII	The "Quaker" Coinage	68
IX	First page of the Fair Minute Book, 1692	101
X	Haggs Level, Nentsberry Mine, Alston	102
XI	Waterwheel at St John's Mine	102
XII	Mine shop at Smallcleugh Mine	135
XIII	Mine tips planted by the London Lead Company	135
XIV	Gadlis Smelt Mill, Flintshire	136
XV	Newcomen pumping engine at Mill Close Mine, Derbyshire	136
XVI	Engineers' Shop	163
XVII	London Lead Company Smelthouse Yard	163
XVIII	Entrance to Haggs Level, Nentsberry Mine	164
XIX	Smelt Mill, Brewery Shaft	164
XX	Nent Head Band	165
XXI	Middleton Hall	165
XXII	Pattinson pans, Nent Head Smelt Mill	166
XXIII	Wheel at Coldberry Mine	166

LINE DRAWINGS

1	Gillgill Lane, Nent Head	19
2	Nent Head Village	21
3	Nent Head Reading Room, School and Under-Manager's House	70
4	The London Lead Company's leases	76
5	Arms of the London Lead Company	107
6	Air blowing machine	144

Let us now praise famous men and our fathers that begat us.

There be of them that have left a name behind them, that their praises might be reported.

And some there be which have no memorial; who are perished as though they had never been; and are become as though they had never been born; and their children after them.

But these were merciful men, whose righteousness hath not been forgotten.

With their seed shall continually remain a good inheritance, and their children are within the covenant.

Their seed standeth fast, and their children for their sakes.

Their seed shall remain for ever, and their glory shall not be blotted out.

Their bodies are buried in peace; but their name liveth for evermore.

ECCLESIASTICUS XLIV

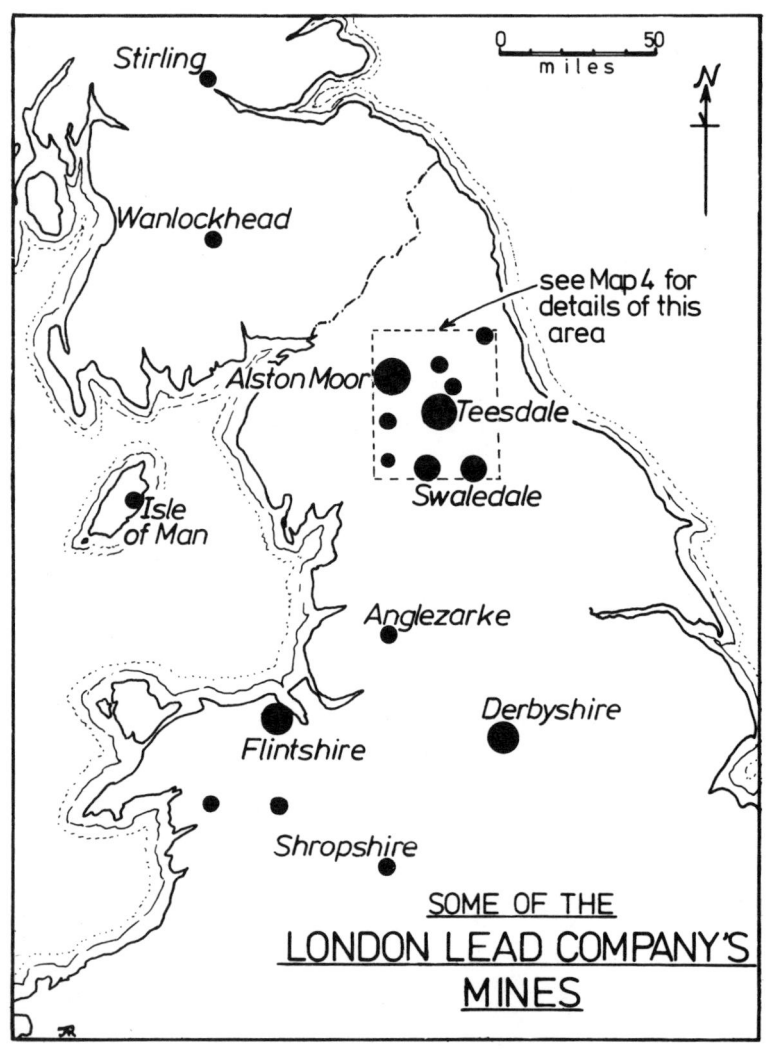

Map 1   The London Lead Company's mines in Britain.

PREFACE

The first edition of this book, published in 1938 by the Friends Historical Society, was an amplified version of the author's Presidential Address to the Society. Since that time there has been a great upsurge in interest in Industrial Archaeology and mining history, and copies of the book have become exceedingly scarce and much sought after. In response to this demand a second edition was published in 1977. Whilst this second edition was largely a facsimile of the original text the author took the opportunity to add another chapter discussing the technical developments made by the London Lead Company. Additional notes and references were added together with a number of new illustrations and plates.

In his introduction to the second edition the author notes that his remarks on the state of the buildings and mines refer to the 1930's and since that date there has been a deterioration in their condition.

With this upsurge in interest in mining history came the formation and expansion of mining history organisations in the 1970's. This led to a broader appreciation of the importance and value of mining remains in the North Pennines, both above and below ground. Long forgotten sites became subject to regular visits, surface remains and underground workings were explored, surveyed and recorded. With this increased activity and interest came the realisation that the remains were deteriorating, sometimes at an alarming rate. Action was obviously required before an important aspect of the North Pennine heritage was lost for ever. Preservation and restoration in the 1970's tended to be carried out by small but dedicated groups of amateur enthusiasts spurred on by the dereliction they saw around them, notable examples of such groups being the Earby Mine Research Group and the Northern Mines Research Society. Restoration at Kilhope, in County Durham saw what was the first significant contribution of public money and resources.

General awareness grew as groups, such as Norpex Mining Research Group, gave talks and organised guided tours for the general public and local authority representatives. With this growing awareness it became clear, in addition to having archaeological value, the mining remains had potential as a tourist attraction. Once again the mines, the legacy of the London Lead Company, could contribute to the local economy and increase employment opportunities. With this prospect in mind the County and District Councils of Cumbria, Northumberland and Durham are now playing an active role in restoration, development of visitor and interpretation facilities, and the seeking of grants to fund the operations. Work has now begun in earnest on several sites and the Kilhope Wheel Mining Centre has opened and is attracting many visitors. The three Counties are adopting a coordinated approach to ensure that all aspects of the mining and its associated industries are incorporated in the programme of restoration and development. Clearly the mines do have a new lease of life, though one which I suspect would come as a considerable surprise to the old miners, were they here to see it!

This story would not be complete without some mention of the North Pennine Heritage Trust. The Trust, established in 1986 was set up to further the conservation, interpretation and restoration of the unique heritage of the Northern Pennines. Based on Alston Moor and with a membership of over 200 local inhabitants, the Trust are working with the other organisations to ensure a future for one of the London Lead Company's main centres of activity. Work has commenced on restoration of the Rampgill-Smallclough complex and plans are well advanced for the development of a mining contre in one of the London Lead Company buildings at Nent Head.

In view of all these activities a third edition of Dr. Raistrick's "Two Centuries" could not have come at a more appropriate time. Several books on the history of mining in the North Pennines have recently been reprinted. However no library would be complete without a copy of this work.

Dr. Raistrick at the age of 92 is an inspiration to all those involved in mining research. The year's have not dulled his memories of Alston Moor. As a young man he spent many years on "The Moor" with Amos Treloar, manager of the Vieille Montagne Company who reworked the mines for zinc ore between the turn of the century and the second world war. Today he is one of the few people who have had the experience of seeing the mines when they were still in operation.

Through his patient researches and his many publications he is recognised as an authority on lead mining in the North Pennines and on the role played by members of the Society of Friends.

Rod. J. Ireland. Norpex Mining Research Group

INTRODUCTION

SOURCES

Many people familiar with the lead mining districts of the North of England must have heard the name "Quaker Company" or "London Lead Company" associated in local tradition with many things, varying from the ownership of now derelict mines to the making of roads or endowment of a school or church. If their interest has been roused to the point of a search for further information about this Company, it is almost certain that little or nothing will have been found, either among the printed records of the Society of Friends (Quakers) or in any of the many works on economic or industrial history.[1] In spite of its very widespread interests and its history of more than two centuries of continuous activities, its records until recently have been remarkably obscure. Few of the families of Friends long connected with the Company as shareholders or as members of the Court of Assistants, seem to have preserved any account of its work, or even to have cherished much in the way of family traditions about the concern.

Through the activity of one of the last members of the Court of Assistants of the Company Henry T. Mennell, and of Dr. H. Louis of Newcastle-on-Tyne, the Minute Books of the Court of Assistants of the Company were preserved from the general destruction of papers at the liquidation of the Company in 1905, and they are now preserved in the Library of the North of England Institute of Mining and Mechanical Engineers, Newcastle-on-Tyne, where during several recent years they have been studied and transcribed by the author. From these, practically our whole knowledge of the Company's business activities is derived. Two other major sources are provided by (*a*) a collection of papers, leases, plans, etc., relating to the Company's activities in Derbyshire, 1721-80, preserved by James Hall Shield of Burnlaw, and for some time clerk of Allendale Friends' Meeting, a descendant of one of the founder families of the Company; and (*b*) an "index" to the letter books of the Company 1816-68, preserved by George H. Mennell and loaned to the author. Minor sources

[1] Numbered notes are collected at the end of each chapter.

of information are found in scattered papers and reports among the records of the Vielle Montagne Zinc Company (Societe des Mines & Fonderies de Zinc de la Vielle Montagne) the successors to the London Lead Company in most of the Alston Moor area, among the Greenwich Hospital records as lessors of part of the London Lead Company's area, and in a small collection of MSS., etc., in the possession of the author. Information on the lives and activities of the early Friends in the Company, apart from their purely business affairs, has largely been supplied by Irene L. Edwards from the records in Friends House Library, and from her own researches into the history of the London Monthly Meetings of the Society of Friends.

The most persistent tradition of the origin of the "Quaker Company", largely sponsored by Edward Pease of Darlington, at the beginning of the nineteenth century, and reaffirmed by Bainbridge (*Twice Seven*, 1933) but entirely unsupported either by the records of the Society of Friends or the minute books of the Company, is that the interest of Friends in lead mining was secured as the result of a concern of two women members of the Society, for the unemployed miners of the north Pennines, towards the end of the seventeenth century. Out of the attempts to rehabilitate the mines arose the "Quaker Lead Company". It is possible that a basis for this tradition could be found for the "Ryton Company" (see later), but it certainly does not apply to the larger Company, the origin of which is clearly set forth in the minute books.

The minute books are entitled "Fair Minute Books of the Court of Assistants of the London Lead Company", and they extend from 1692 to 1899 with only one volume missing, apart from the last one, 1899 to 1905. Those now preserved are thirty-seven large folio volumes varying from 250 to 400 pages a volume, comprising in all a record of nearly 13,000 meetings of the Court. There are in addition to these three volumes of "General Court Minutes" which are entirely formal and record only the annual appointment of Governor, Court, etc., and apportionment of dividends, one volume of "Minutes of the Committee of the Royal Mines Copper"[*]

---

[*] "The Proprietors of the Royal Mines Copper & other works vested in Wm. Monsen, Wm. Thomson Esq. etc. as Trustees" is the fuller title of this committee; see notice in *The Postman*, November 1st, 1701.

1697-1704, a volume of mine reports relating to Nent Head (Alston district) in the early nineteenth century, and three volumes of plans.

From a close study of the minutes it is clear that the life of the Company can be allocated to five main phases :—

(1) 1692-1704. The period of the " Royal Mines Copper " and the " Ryton Company ", with the first period, 1692-5, of the " Governor and Company for Smelting Down Lead with Pitt Coal and with Sea Coal " (easier referred to as " the Bristol Company ").

(2) 1704-10. First period of the consolidated " Quaker Company " (known by its minute book title, and among business records in general, as " the London Lead Company ").

(3) 1710-90. Period of widest expansion with mines in all parts of the British Isles.

(4) 1790-1882. Consolidation as a Northern Company, and period of greatest social activity.

(5) 1882-1905. Closing period of the Company.

In this account of the Company, interest will be mainly focused upon its social activities during the fourth period, the late eighteenth and the nineteenth centuries, in the northern districts of the Pennines, where the concentration of their mining and smelting works from about 1750 onwards brought together a large population in an area that was almost without roads and markets, and with tiny hamlets and isolated farms only sufficient for a small population. When the Company began its period of expansion and accepted a somewhat paternal responsibility for the area, the old hamlets were extended into villages, a new village (Nent Head) designed and built, and social services supplied to meet the various needs of the new community.

The principal factor that enabled the Company to undertake this very extensive responsibility, was its great stability by which it weathered all the difficulties of two critical centuries. Its stability was based on very sound technical processes in mining and smelting, constantly kept up to date, and a readiness to spend money on experiment and development. This policy will be discussed in a later part of the book. The control of all affairs of the Company was in the hands of a Governor and Court of twenty-four

Assistants, elected annually, and meeting every Tuesday in London (at 9 Martin's Lane, Cannon Street), and regularly appointing sub-committees for special purposes. The Court sent a " deputation " of some of its members, usually four, including the Governor or Deputy Governor, to visit all the mining areas, at fairly regular intervals, to maintain personal contact with its officials and employees. In each principal area there was a Superintendent or General Manager under whom worked a number of District Agents, Cashier, Smelting and Washing Agents, etc. Work of every kind, technical and social, was carried out by the local superintendent and agents after approval by the Court, and consequently most of the local activities are noted in abstract in the Court minute books.

Friends had been interested in mines in the Alston Moor district at least as early as 1696 through the Ryton Company (detailed in a later chapter), which became part of the London Lead Company in 1705. The Company quickly extended its interest into the valley of the Derwent around Blanchland, and sought to extend the area of its leases around Alston, but had only a few mines working until about 1750. Their greatest expansion in the district was indirectly the result of political action following the Jacobite rebellion of 1715. One of the leading figures of the rebellion in the North was the Earl of Derwentwater, holder of the manor of Alston Moor and many adjoining estates. He was executed for his share in the rising and his estates were confiscated to the Crown.* After some delay they were granted to Greenwich Hospital along with all manorial and mineral rights.

These estates included a great part of Tynedale and of Alston Moor, where the Company already held a number of scattered mines. The policy of the Greenwich Hospital Commissioners was at first to offer for public tender the separate lease of each mine in their area, but from about

* A despatch from Lieutenant Maughan to Captain Clavering, both King's Officers, says a man was sent from Dilston by Lady Derwentwater to " one Charles Allsopp's, in East Allen, who buys the Lord's lead or ore, with a letter, and he went immediately and brought a great bagg of gold, and sent with the messenger £150, and said he thought his Lordship would have sent for more ". Charles Allsopp was the manager and chief smelter for the London Lead Company, in the North, living then at Whitfield in Allendale.

1740 to 1750 this policy proved expensive and very unsatisfactory. In 1750 the London Lead Company were allowed to take up a large block of the Hospital leases around the head of the Nent valley (tributary to the South Tyne, joining it at Alston) and to extend one of their earlier mining leases, Priorsdale in the South Tyne, Garrigill district, to run coterminous with Nent Head. To these large blocks of leases, were added between 1757 and 1765, other areas that made the Company the proprietors of most of the Alston Moor mining field. This was the greatest factor of all in developing the social side of the Company's work, as it put them very soon in the position of employers of a population of many hundreds of miners' families, in an area almost unprovided with houses, villages, and all the sheer necessities of a community.

This expansion in the North was well established when the Welsh and Derbyshire concerns of the Company began to experience their difficulties, and was the basic factor in the decision to close them down. The mine leases surrendered elsewhere were replaced by equivalent leases in Alston Moor, Weardale and Teesdale, thus producing the remarkably large but compact northern grouping of the nineteenth century. By 1760 the Company had so many miners drawn together on the Nent Head leases that they created their village of Nent Head, and because of the isolation of the area, gradually provided themselves all social services, schools, chapels, shops, houses, etc., and thus entered on their greatest period of social experiment. The Alston Moor mines were continued until 1882, when the Company, for many reasons, decided to restrict its activities to Teesdale, and accepted an offer to purchase the Alston Moor estates and leases, mines, mills, etc., at a valuation. They were finally sold for £30,562 7s. 7d. to a company, Cammeron, Swan & Company of Newcastle, which resold in 1896 to the present holders, the Vielle Montagne Zinc Company (Societe des Mines & Fonderies de Zinc de la Vielle Montagne) of Belgium, who in many ways are following the traditions of the Quaker Company as good employers with a " live " social conscience.

The Teesdale area, the last home of the London Lead Company, was only developed in their latest periods of activity ; the first lease was taken in 1753, of a small group of mines at Newbiggin, near Middleton-in-Teesdale, followed in 1771 by the lease of the mines and smelt mill at Egglestone, a few miles lower down the valley. Egglestone was made the smelting centre for Teesdale, with a group of three smelt mills, and Middleton became the office centre of the Company and, after about 1850, the residence of the northern agent. When the Derwent mines (Blanchland, etc.) were drawing towards their end about 1800, the Company took up leases of mines and smelt mills at Stanhope in Weardale, and at Bollihope, a tributary valley of Weardale, which were put in operation in 1806, when work was finally closed down in the Derwent valley. The Weardale mines and estates were linked with Teesdale, while further estates at Hilton, Murton, and Dufton, near Appleby, Westmorland, and at Lunehead, near Brough (the mines are actually in Yorkshire) were added to Nent Head and Alston Moor.

This northern district has been mentioned in some detail as it was the scene of most of the Company's social activity. It occupies an area of nearly 1,200 square miles of mountainous country, lying within the triangle between the towns of Hexham, Penrith, and Darlington, and being the northern end of the Pennines. The area is mainly rough moorland, much of it over 2,000 feet above sea level, with deep-cut valleys and steep fell sides. It is a land of steep slopes with rocky crags, and wild moorland bogs, with isolated farms and hamlets at heights that are very unusual in this country. The principal " town " is Alston, at the beginning of the nineteenth century a market village, the centre of a very extensive parish covering most of Alston Moor. The total number of inhabited houses at the census of 1811 was, for Alston Moor, 461, but they housed over 1,000 families. The main street of Alston rises with dangerous steepness from 950 feet to 1,100 feet above sea level. Nent Head village is built on a steep hillside between 1,460 feet and 1,600 feet O.D. In Teesdale, Middleton is comparatively low at 800 feet O.D. The mines and mine " shops " at which the miners lived during the week, are much higher—Ashgill Head *Low* Shop is at 1,900 feet O.D., Teesdale and Hardshins are above 1,800 feet O.D., while the mines range up to various heights between 1,500 feet and 2,500 feet O.D. The roads that the Company built across the fells from valley to valley, cross the fells at passes many of which are very high—Nent Head to Garrigill road, 1,940 feet O.D. ; Garrigill to Middleton road, 1,950 feet O.D. ; Garrigill to Murton and Hilton road, 2,460 feet O.D. ; Nent Head to Stanhope road, 2,056 feet O.D. It must be remembered that this is an area of high rainfall (about 80 inches per annum) and that it is no uncommon experience even nowadays for the villages of the area to be " snowbound " for considerable periods.

The minutes of the Court record the receipt of many letters which throw some light on the wild weather experienced in the North, and the effect of storms on the continuance of the work. The following may be taken as illustrative examples :—

24.1.1820   Most intense frost known for years. Washing floors etc. stopped as water courses are all frozen.
4.3.1822   Great floods in Westmorland have washed away all bridges on the mine roads.
8.2.1823   Most severe snow and frost suspended work.
18.10.1825   Most unprecedented drought stopped all washing.
15.11.1825   A heavy snow storm—the most adverse season we have ever known.
7.6.1830   Very heavy floods with damage particularly at Skears.
26.12.1836-2.1.1837   Very severe snowstorms have stopped all work. All roads impassable.
1846   Very considerable floods this winter have carried away nearly all our bridges.
1853 and 1855   very heavy snow storms reported on several occasions throughout these two winters, followed by floods which damaged roads and bridges and washing floors.
1.11.1859 to 8.2.1860   continued snowstorms and blizzards have stopped all work.

and so the record goes on, every two or three years, roads and bridges destroyed, washing floors and water wheels overthrown, or the men laid off work because water is either frozen up or there is a drought. One of the greatest difficulties was that of transport of food to the miners in the higher villages, and the continued inspection of the mines by the agents.

Partly to meet the very real difficulty of the miners getting to and from the remoter mines to their homes, the system of " Mine Shops " was introduced in 1818. The "shop" was a very substantially built cottage near the mine mouth, fitted with rough bunk beds, cooking range, and a few simple necessities, such that a few miners could with considerable comfort live in it during the week, walking home on Saturday and returning Monday morning. A great many of these shops were built, and the miners on several occasions sent a resolution of very warm thanks to the Court for the great comfort of them. Where they were not needed for lodging miners, they were still built as changing and drying houses, and are a characteristic part of the mining landscape.

Notes

[1] The principal accounts of the Company will be found in the following :—

Wallace, W. "Alston Moor : its Pastoral People : its Mines and Miners ; from earliest times to recent times." Newcastle-on-Tyne. 1890.

Bainbridge. "Twice Seven." 1933. The references here are to the later period of the Company in Teesdale, and are sketchy and contain many serious inaccuracies.

Raistrick, A. "The London Lead Company, 1692-1905." *Trans. Newcomen Society for the History of Engineering and Technology*, Vol. XIV, 1935. A history of the leases and technical aspects of the Company.

Raistrick, A. "Lead Mining and Smelting in the Northern Pennines in the Eighteenth and Nineteenth Centuries." *Proc. University of Durham Phil. Soc.*, 1936. This discusses the work of both the London Lead Company and the Allendale mines, in lead smelting and silver refining.

Raistrick, A. "Mill Close Lead Mine, Derbyshire." *Proc. University of Durham Phil. Soc.*, 1937. An account of the London Lead Company in Derbyshire, 1721-80.

Raistrick, A. *Quakers in Science and Industry*, 1950, for general background, and chapter V, "The Mining Companies".

Raistrick, A. and Jennings, B. *A History of Lead Mining in the Pennines*, 1965.

Bevan-Evans, M. "Gadlis and Flintshire Lead-Mining in the eighteenth century", *Journal of the Flintshire Historical Society*. XVIII, 1960, 75-130; XIX, 1961, 32-60; XX, 1962, 58-89. A fuller account of the Welsh affairs.

Plans and papers in the author's collection of mining manuscripts along with miscellaneous letters, papers and plans relating to the London Lead Company and to other mining companies.

CHAPTER I

Housing of the Workpeople—Building of Nent Head Village—Gardens and Allotments—Food in the Famine Years of Nineteenth Century—The Corn Association.

DURING the first hundred years of the London Lead Company the minutes contain a surprisingly large number of examples of the benevolent and wise outlook of the agents employed and empowered by the Court, to represent the Company in each area. As, however, the mines were widely scattered, as has been seen, over most of the British Isles, efforts towards the relief of poverty, or provision of miners' houses, etc., were necessarily sporadic, called forth more by particular circumstances and incidents in the different districts than by any vital policy of the Company. With the end of the eighteenth century, however, all the conditions were changed. The Company consolidated itself in the North of England, and rapidly drew together a community of nearly four thousand people more or less directly dependent on them for livelihood, in an area where there were no previous provisions of shelter and services, for such a community. In 1753 the Company had faced the implication of its new leases in the Nent valley, by designing and building an entirely new village, Nent Head, about five miles south-east of Alston, and had thus become landlords in all senses of the word. This first village was small, with a few well-planned, solidly-built houses for the smelters and officials attached to the Nent Head mills, but most of the miners were actually enabled to lodge at small farms and cottages scattered over the fells all around the Moor. The Company gave considerable time to enlarging and improving many of the farms, making room for the lodging of miners as well as farm hands, and providing for the care of the miners' children in both day and Sunday schools. The great increase in mining population was not really serious, however, until after the sale in 1792 of the other properties of the Company in Wales and Derbyshire, and the subsequent taking of additional leases in the Alston Moor and Teesdale areas. By 1815 this expansion of population was almost at its peak, and the

Company were compelled to define very clearly their policy as landlords as well as employers. The smaller experiments initiated shortly after the building of Nent Head, were the basis of this new policy, and it will be of interest to note how far this policy in some ways reflects the spirit of the age in which it was formed, and in other ways is far in advance of that age. The period between 1800 and 1860 or 1870 can be taken as the best period of the social activities of the Company, for by 1870 many of the Company's main services had been recognized and partly or wholly taken over by the State. About 1800 the Company perhaps reflected the feelings of the period most slavishly, in their rather pathetic belief in a narrow education as a cure for all moral weaknesses of their workmen. Education was to teach the men their " duty " and keep them respectful and loyal to the Company's interests, but at the same time, many advanced experiments were made that more than compensate for a rather marked " patronage " of the workmen by the agents and Court. They were far in advance of the age not only in provision of day schools for all the children of the district, but in their recognition of the value and necessity for recreations of divers types—bands, cricket clubs, libraries, lectures, gardens, allotments, etc. etc., and the inevitable provision of work times that would enable miners to enjoy all these recreational facilities. There is a very modern flavour about their " welfare " work. They were seriously concerned for the health of their workpeople and their families, and besides providing medical staff and workman's fund, etc., realized that health must be based on good housing, good and adequate water supply, sanitation, and the provision of baths and wash houses. On the matter of wages, the policy of the Company is a mixture of keen business and concern for a maintained standard of living, without excessively high wage rates. Perhaps the spirit of the age, already referred to peeps out in the report of an agent in 1800, that " we have reduced wages below the excessive figures prevailing last year and in consequence have reformed the morals of the miners—intemperance has ceased and their lavish and extravagant habits are corrected ! " Against this we have decisions reached as early as 1802 that the " bargains (that is the quarterly bargain for the rate of pay related mainly to a piece rate) are to be made independent of the price of lead and calculated to give a regular weekly wage, if necessary to be increased so as always to be equal to their support and comfort, and further, the price of food must always be taken into account, and special subsidies in money and through the Corn Association given in times of scarcity."

In 1753 the story of Nent Head village begins with the extension of the Nent Head smelt mill and mine buildings and the building of a group of cottages close to them, at a place where, for a short distance the valley floor of the Nent widens a little. Near the mill a small estate, Cherry Tree

Fig 1   Part of Nent Head from Gillgill Lane.

Hill, was bought from the Alston Brewery Company for £990 and on it a new house built for the Agent of the mines, which, after sixty years was rebuilt just as it still stands. (See Plate I.) The house is still the home of the mines manager and agent and retains yet some of the furniture provided by the Company in 1816. The offices of the Company were at first in the upper part of the village on the bank of the Gillgill Burn which runs through the village, but at the rebuilding of the house on Cherry Tree Hill, the offices were transferred there, and built on to the end of the manager's house, where they still are. Large gardens, a small field, a cottage, and a large plantation were added to the house to form a neat little estate. By 1840 the Company had spent over £2,200 on buildings and improvements on the Cherry Tree Hill estate. The village of Nent Head took shape at the junction of the Gillgill Burn and the river Nent, where the Alston to Weardale track crosses the Nent. The earliest cottages were near the smelt mills and along the side of the tributary stream, the Gillgill Burn, but by 1820 these had become quite inadequate. Many old cottages and farms in bad repair had been bought and rebuilt, but a more extensive and co-ordinated plan was needed if all the officials and workpeople of the Company were to be housed comfortably. In 1825 a new and larger village was planned, with thirty-five cottages, clock tower, market hall, school and chapel, etc., set in a large acreage of fields, gardens and plantations, and its building proceeded apace at a cost of about £3,000. Rents for the cottages were £4 to £6 a year and all were provided with gardens, which later became of considerable importance under the care and stimulus of the local Horticultural Society—a remarkable achievement when it is remembered that the lowest part of the village is above 1,450 feet above sea level, and the rainfall about 60-70 inches per year. In the new village area land was given as a site for a Methodist Chapel, and much later, in 1843, further land was given for a Church of England and a house built for the vicar. The old inn of the village, the Miners' Arms, was purchased in 1823 and on several occasions its rent was reduced as its trade was diminishing, "the miners preferring books to drink", as the report says. The inn was rebuilt with much more accommodation for travellers and less for drinking.

The village had a Ready Money Store which, by wise purchase through the Company of large stocks of goods for resale, was soon a great success, and with its success the credit dealers were considerably reduced in number and power. During later years the village was improved in many ways, a post office built in 1848, a proper water supply laid on in 1850, baths and a public wash house provided in 1865, and about the same time the old 1750-60 cottages rebuilt. School, church, chapels, etc., were all added, the sites being given by the Company and large donations made towards the buildings and endowments. (See Fig. 2.)

BUILDING OF THE NENT HEAD VILLAGE

The centre of the village was formed by a fairly wide open space of level ground, between the river Nent and the steep fell side on which most of the houses were built. At the foot of the slope were the smelters' and overmen's houses, with the Surgeon's and Mill Agents' houses at the south end; after these came the inn, then the Chapel, and a small area later occupied by the Reading Room and Library. In front of these lay the Alston-Stanhope road crossing a wide open space, then all the area from the road to the bank of the river Nent was laid out as the Rampgill Low washing floor.

Fig 2 The centre of Nent Head village. Right to left: wash house and baths, clock tower, market hall, ready money shop and warehouse. All pulled down by 1905.

On the side of the floor towards the road stood, first at the south end, the warehouse and Ready Money shop, with the Market House next to them. This was a fairly large building with large arched entrance in the middle and a through road passing from this arch to the back of the building, where was a yard and stables. The front and back entrances were closed with wrought-iron gates, and gave rise to the local wit's name of the " Lion House ", which is still remembered in the village. On each side of the through alley were a series of partitioned and fitted stalls, where visiting butchers, farmers and tradesmen could set out their stocks on market day. Just behind, but rising high above the market building, was the Clock Tower, with a four-faced clock visible from all parts of the village and the washing floors. The clock works, faces, and the masonry of the tower are still carefully preserved in the mine stores, and it has been suggested that they might on a suitable occasion be re-erected somewhere in the village centre as a memorial. (See Fig. 3).

Next to the Market Hall was the School House, to accommodate 200 children though, judging from its size on the plan, they must have been rather crowded. In 1864 a new and improved School was built up the hillside and about the middle of the village, on the site indicated on the plan. This new School has a finely-proportioned hall in a rather ecclesiastical style of architecture, with an annex of smaller rooms built out as a wing to the main block. All the rooms are very well proportioned and of striking appearance. In 1896 the County Authority built a new elementary school just outside the old village area, on a site tucked away between the mine dumps, and down towards the riverside. After 1896 the second school building after many vicissitudes became the village Assembly Hall, and is now well used for concerts, dances, meetings, etc. In the main hall, and over the doorway to the wing, is a well-cut marble tablet to Robert Stagg, the agent at the time of building.

The inscription is as follows :—

TESTIMONIAL

TO ROBERT STAGG ESQ. FOR UPWARDS OF TWENTY FIVE YEARS SUPERINTENDENT OF THE LEAD COMPANY'S WORKS ; IN RECOGNITION OF HIS INDEFATIGABLE LABOURS TO PROMOTE THE GENERAL INTERESTS OF THE COMPANY, AND THE WELFARE OF THE NUMEROUS BODY OF WORKMEN COMMITTED TO HIS CARE ; MORE ESPECIALLY FOR THE INVALUABLE SERVICE RENDERED BY HIM IN ORIGINATING IN THE YEAR 1818 THE FORMATION OF THE SCHOOLS, TO THE USE OF WHICH THIS BUILDING IS DEDICATED.
ERECTED BY ORDER OF THE GOVERNOR AND THE COURT OF ASSISTANTS PERSUANT TO A RESOLUTION PASSED UNANIMOUSLY AT A COURT HELD IN LONDON ON THE VIII NOVEMBER
MDCCCLX

After the building of the second school, the old school rooms, adjoining the Market Hall, were converted to new uses and were able to continue their useful career as part of the social centre of the village. One room in the upper storey, and nearest the Market Hall, was set apart as the " Band Room ", the home and practice room of the village band, about which something will be said later. The rest of the building was extended and, with certain structural alterations, was made into a public wash house and baths. A boiler house was added, to supply steam and hot water to the whole building. In the bath house there were a number of ordinary baths as well as shower baths, with hot and cold water to all of them, and soap and towels, and the use of the baths could be had by anyone at a charge of one penny. The care of the baths and the boiler house was usually in the hands of a man either with a slight disablement or approaching retiring age, and the job was generally regarded as a half retirement, with a prominent public position. In the wash house, the main room was equipped with sixteen large tubs and corresponding boiling vats, supplied with steam and hot water. To each set of tub and boiler belonged rubbing boards and all necessary equipment, including a mechanical stirrer or " posser " operated by a handle at the side of the tub. A bank of steam-heated drying cupboards was on the opposite side of the room, and each tub had its own cupboard, with a five-rank rack that wheeled in and out on rails and wheels. In addition to these sixteen individual sets, there were folding tables, and two huge box mangles for general use. Each woman in the village had her wash day allocated, and paid one penny for the day's use of the place and apparatus. The clothes were not only washed, but completely dried and mangled, and the older people still remember that most women, starting at 9 a.m., were able to complete their washing and take home the clean, dried and finished clothes by 6 p.m. the same day. This wash house remained in use until 1905, and the lower part of the building was incorporated about 1910 in the magnetic separator house connected with the new washing plant then erected. This lower portion of the original school house is the only survivor of the public buildings on the low side of the road.

The Rampgill Low washing floor, between these buildings and the river, was redesigned in 1818, with a large crushing mill for the ore, and was connected by light rail waggon ways with the various mine levels near by. From the crushing rollers the ore was taken through various washing places, buddles, hotching tubs, etc., to be separated from the rock and unprofitable spar, in preparation for the smelt mill. It was on the washing floors both here and the adjoining

Rampgill High floor, that many of the boys were employed, and it was here that the women clamoured in crowds for work, during the hungry years of 1817 and 1818. These washing floors at the centre of the village must always have presented a busy and strange scene to anyone not familiar with the processes of ore dressing. Near the exit from the mine level lies the great dump of " deads ", i.e. stone and shale brought from " cross cuts " and other tunnels cut through non-productive strata. The railways from the level mouth run in two divergent sets, one on to the dead heaps and the other running on a staging across a long series of stone partitioned bunkers, the " bouse teams ", where the bouse, i.e. the ore bearing stuff, is tipped. From the bouse teams, the bouse is carried to the picking floors, where clean ore lumps are taken out by hand, and the rest comes forward to the crushers. Picture, just behind the market hall and shop, a 40-feet diameter water wheel, turning the crushing rollers through which the loads of bouse pass with a crunching roar and rattle. (See Plate II.) The crushed bouse passes out on to the sloping "buddles", either sloping water-washed stone tables or the later circular buddles, with stirrer paddles, etc. Here the running water effects some separation of material, ore from rock. The larger material was again hand-picked, and the finer stuff sent on to the hotching tubs where, either by hand or by simple mechanical contrivance, the stuff is shaken up in water, on a sieve, and further separations made. The final clean ore, crushed down to a coarse powder, goes to the " bing steads " ready for transference to the furnaces. All over the washing floor are boys and men hard at work, breaking, washing, and wheeling bouse, streams of " slimes " running off into settling pools so that the last finest fragments of ore can be trapped—everywhere noise, running water, and boys. It must always have made the centre of the village appear as a hive of industry.

Some of the Company's earliest leases had lain in the piece of country between Nent Head and the valley of the South Tyne, in the area known as Priorsdale, and this area was more accessible from Garrigill than from Nent Head—hence the Company at quite an early date took an interest in Garrigill and its development. In 1798 they purchased the corn mill, 140 acres of ground, two houses, and sundry cottages, and further cottages were built to house the men brought on to the new leases in Priorsdale. In Garrigill some of the early experiments were made with smallholdings, small cottages being built with up to six acres of enclosed land attached, in addition to rights on a fifty-acre pasture. During the Company's interest in Garrigill, they provided money and a site for a Girls' School, a Parsonage, a Wesleyan Chapel and a Primitive Methodist Chapel, and built a Library, provided the salary for a curate, and also presented a harmonium to the church. Drainage and adequate water supply were also provided, and all old property on their estate was either pulled down and replaced by new, or reconditioned.

The Priorsdale estate was purchased about 1820 for £7,300,* and the few farms and buildings on it reconditioned and a road built through it from Nent Head to Garrigill. 510 acres of ground here were planted with timber at an early date, and further plantings added before 1882 when the estates were sold. A nursery was established for young trees, and provided a constant supply of young seedling trees for the other estates.

In Westmorland, at Dufton and Hilton, a similar procedure was followed—land was purchased, an agent's and smelters' houses were built, and old cottages mostly pulled down and new ones built on their sites. Water supply in every case was a prime concern of the Company. Along with the physical comforts of good housing and gardens and water, the spiritual welfare of the miners was catered for by the gift of sites for, and contributions towards, churches and chapels, and provision by the Company of schools and libraries.

The second largest estate of the Company was at Middleton-in-Teesdale, purchased and built in 1815, on rather similar lines to Nent Head, the plan, of course, being made to fit the local ground and the rather smaller area. During the Company's first fifty years at Middleton over 100 cottages were built and many houses and farms rebuilt. Like Nent Head, offices, school, chapels, a clock tower, etc., were provided to form a nucleus for the estate. After 1880 Middleton became the head office of the Company and the

* Report in 1824 says, " A flat of ore has been discovered in Ashgill Mine, Priorsdale, which has yielded profits that put the Company in gratuitous possession of the estate."

residence of the agent and general manager. At Middleton the prime conditions, however, were different from Nent Head. Middleton-in-Teesdale is an old village with a church and free school dating back for many centuries, and the new town built by the Company was simply a suburb to this old village, the shops, market and church serving the new population as well as the old. The Company, however, followed its customary procedure, providing first cottages and gardens, then baths, Company schools, chapels, and all the social amenities that the old village did not possess. In the first forty years of the nineteenth century the Company spent on land for the villages £23,809, and on buildings £34,409, in the areas just mentioned. The portion of Middleton built by the Company is described by a contemporary writer as follows :—

Masterman Place or as it is sometimes called, *New Middleton*, was erected in 1833 by the London Lead Company from the chaste and appropriate design of Mr. Bonomi, and under the direction of Robert Stagg. It consists of several uniform rows of neat and convenient cottages, situated in a spacious garden, a portion of which was appropriated to each dwelling. The increasing population of Middleton had considerably enhanced the rents of dwelling houses there, and it was to diminish this burden that the Company built Masterman Place, in which, as vacancies occur, they place their most deserving workmen, thus combining general utility with the reward of personal merit. The first occupiers took possession of their new abodes in May 1824, accompanied by bands of music, etc. The rent of each cottage and garden is £4 per annum.

The result of this policy was that the Company's workpeople in all their mining localities were well housed, and were fully provided with social and educational amenities such as few other villages in the area possess even to-day. Time after time the agents report that their workpeople are content at a time when rioting and striking were common in other parts of the same mining field and throughout the country, and they ascribe this partly to the influence of the Sunday schools and partly to the general care the Company show for the physical wellbeing of their workmen. In the absence of most of the report books and letters, one can only quote occasional items from Court minutes and index :—

GARDENS AND ALLOTMENTS

REPORT BOOK OF DEPUTATIONS.

Nov. 1816   Testimony to the good conduct of the men when the neighbouring miners are all dissatisfied.

1818   Miners express their thanks to the Court for many acts of kindness, for the provision of "shops" and most particularly for the provision of schools.

1824   Deputations to express thanks for cottages, "they knew not before what comfort meant".

1830   Great present distress, but good conduct of the miners very marked. "Cannot be spoiled by the vile example setting by the Labourers in the South."

1831   "In these times of agitation, the spirit of the Company's workmen was never better."

1838   Great dearness of provisions, corn supplied by the Company.

1838 Dec.   The conduct of the miners reflects the highest credit on them as men and Christians.
The only complaint received was that the temperance society had ruined the inn (at Nent Head).

1847   Great distress amongst the whole population consequent on sickness and high price of provisions—general expression of thanks for the sympathy and constant assistance from the Company.

A writer in 1834 says of the Middleton district :—

The beneficial effects of the regulations adopted by the London Lead Company toward their workmen, are strikingly apparent in the general decorum and good behaviour visible in Middleton. Drunkenness and quarrelling are punished by dismissal, and in other respects a strict but salutary discipline is preserved.

The Company's interest in gardens is shown in the way in which every cottage that they built on any of their estates was provided with a garden adjoining, and in the many ways in which they fostered the love of gardens among the workpeople. At an early date a Horticultural Society was formed at Nent Head, and a similar one at Middleton, to both of which the Company were generous subscribers. Later, similar societies were founded at Garrigill and in Westmorland, for Dufton and Hilton. Prizes were offered each year by the Company for the two best cultivated gardens on each estate ; at first each prize was 10s. 6d., but later this was increased to £2 2s. As demand for land in addition to the cottage gardens increased, the Company instructed its agents to purchase small lots of ground from half an acre to two or three acres, in suitable positions, and to let these out to their workpeople in allotments, at rentals varying from 2s. 6d. to 10s. a year. The societies had annual shows of fruit, flowers and vegetables, at which practically every person from manager down to the horse boys showed something or other. In the replanned villages of Nent Head and Middleton-in-Teesdale, about 1820, the average garden supplied to the smallest cottages was about 350 square yards and to the larger cottages, for overmen, under managers, schoolmaster and other officials, about 700 square yards. In addition to these there were about sixteen acres of land for small allotments.

Along with the gardening the Company developed a keen interest in the improvement of pasture land by draining and liming, making many experiments on the high level moors up to 2,000 feet above sea level, and from time to time the agents reported considerable success with this double treatment. This work was of great importance when they adopted the practice of building cottages with considerable enclosures of land and pasture, to form smallholdings. In a similar attempt to utilize and improve some of the abundant high level moorland that they possessed, the Company spent a great deal of time and money on planting the moors with useful timber. Two main methods were adopted, plain planting, and planting after the ground had been partially ploughed and ridged; and the second method proved the better. By 1840 in the Nent Head district, over 650 acres were planted with Scotch fir and some larch, and all the timber needed for the mines was being cut in their own woods. At a later period, many of the old mine dumps were planted from the nurseries, and to-day they are often one of the most attractive features of the rather wild countryside, with their evergreen trees making lovely splashes of dark green colour against the browns of the moors. (See Plate III.)

Some attempts at planting were made when the estates were first purchased, but it was not until the Enclosure Acts for Alston Moor and Priorsdale were obtained in 1815 that extensive and systematic experiments were made, and the plantations became a success. The following minutes will illustrate the progress of the work :—

1815 Alston Moor allotments now enclosed and planted.
1816 About 6 acres more planted this Spring.
1817 Failure of the early plantation is noted.
1818 25 acres are to be planted with Scotch Fir.

The early plantation mentioned here was one of thirty-eight acres on which were planted 110,000 larch and Scotch fir; the cost of enclosing and planting the allotment is given as about £700.

1820 The Alston Moor plantations have a more promising appearance.
1821 Observe very considerable growth in the plants.
1822 Rapid growth is noted in the Guddamgill and Middleton plantations, and Littlegill (part of Priorsdale) is to be similarly enclosed and planted.
1824 A planter, John Thompson, is appointed for Priorsdale at 20/- a week wages.
1825 Middleton plantations are flourishing. The thinnings this year have been valued to the mines at £50.
1826 Where the planting has been done by contract, it is not looking so well. On Alston Moor at Guddamgill (down the valley from Nent Head) the trees die when their roots reach the blue clay.
Middleton plantation thinnings this year are worth to the mines £140.
1827 A nursery plantation for seedling plants to be formed in Priorsdale.
1831 The nursery plantation has fully answered its purpose, but the planter must be dismissed for continued negligence. Middleton plantations flourish.
The plantations around Nent Head House make a thriving appearance.
1834 The 500 acres planted in Priorsdale will soon become of the greatest value.
1835 Growth at Middleton so rapid the plantings may soon be called a wood.

Until 1839 the yearly report is that all plantations except Guddamgill are thriving and growth is very quick. The thinnings are steadily becoming of greater value in the mines.

1839 Priorsdale plantations suffered destruction of many trees by hurricane, January 7th, last.
Plantations in Littlegill failed entirely from same cause as Guddamgill.

1840 Extent of our present plantations is as follows :—
    82 acres by the Tyne, thriving.
    75 ,, Eshgill Burn side looking very well.
    7½ ,, Shield Close are thriving.
    146 ,, Littlegill may be a failure.
    200 ,, ridged on the high ground, may be doubtful.

The system of ridging on the high ground has most surprisingly proved a great success, is a later note :—

1841 From Priorsdale 4220 feet of timber useful in the mines, has been cut. The plantations particularly on the higher ground look well.

Until 1850 again all reports are enthusiastic, and the Company were supplying all their needs of timber from their own woods.

1850 Priorsdale and the whole of Alston Moor has suffered severe injury from a late frost in Spring, the Larch suffering the most.
1851 Priorsdale has suffered this year from the ravages of a Blight among the Larches.

By 1852 the Court considered their scheme of planting as being well established, and cease to minute progress, being assured from time to time by the agents that the concern now grows all its own timber for all purposes. There is no doubt that their plantations to-day remain at most unusual heights. Around Nent Head House at present, a small plantation contains oak at over 1,500 feet above sea level, while in front of the house is a large and beautiful Aurocaria, about 40 feet high, again thriving in their garden plantation at 1,500 feet above sea level.

Throughout the history of the Company, the question of price and adequacy of the food supplies available for their miners had been brought to the consideration of the Court by sheer force of circumstances. The remoteness of many of the mining fields from large markets had subjected the miners to scarcity, both real and artificially stimulated for profit, and on many occasions through the first century of their work the Court authorized the sending from London to Chester, or Wanlock Head, or Alston, of a cargo of food, mainly grain, corn and rice, that was to be sold to the men at London prices.¹ This action was, however, only taken occasionally on specific complaints from the agents, and demanded no settled policy of the Company.

Towards the end of the eighteenth century the general trend of prices throughout the country was marked by a sharp upward movement, with resulting increasing poverty of the labouring classes everywhere. A crisis was reached about 1795, when an acute shortage of food was experienced in all parts of the country. In that year the Court of the Company was informed by its agents of widespread distress among the miners of the North because of the dearness of bread and their remoteness from markets, and the Court began a series of contributions of £50 to be used for the relief of poor miners. Occasional cargoes of grain were sent to Newcastle, and the agents were authorized to buy further stores of grain in Newcastle and Alston markets, to be resold to their employees at cost price. By 1800, however, the position had become very serious, and the Company had to reconsider its responsibilities and decide on some definite line of action to meet the increasing distress and consequent illness and discontent among the population of Alston Moor and Teesdale. An enquiry proved the main source of distress to be the dearness of bread, resulting partly from the scarcity of corn but very largely aggravated by the exorbitant charges of the corn millers and flour dealers. Time after time the workmen had complained of this, until the Company felt that they must find some real solution other than occasional charity. They finally decided in 1800 to buy the old lead mill and engine at Tynebottom, near Garrigill, and to refit it as a corn mill, to supply the whole district. The mill was worked under their supervision, and quite quickly reports were received by the Court that the whole district was benefiting by better ground corn and by just prices. The second source of complaint was that corn had to be brought by the dealers from Newcastle market, which none of the miners were able to visit (a distance of about forty miles), and that the prices were increased almost to prohibitive monopoly levels. The Court ordered the agent at Nent Head to purchase £500 worth of grain, to store it somewhere in the offices, and to sell it to the miners and their families at cost price only. Eight casks of rice were sent from London to supplement this. Along with the operation of the Company's corn mill at Tynebottom, this relieved the situation for the time being, but soon other problems arose. It was difficult to provide this relief for the Company's workmen and see the general population of the district still in the grip of prohibitive prices, so the scheme was soon enlarged and thrown open to all the residents in the district, whether employed in the mines or not.

The form of wages in the mines at this time was the usual one of quarterly " bargains ", in which the agent would each quarter give notice of the veins and places that were to be worked, and ask for offers of prices at which the miners would work the place for so much per fathom of ground cut, or for so much per bing* of ore produced. The intimate knowledge of the ground that each miner or group of miners had, was balanced against the price of lead, and a " bargain " made for the rate of pay for the following quarter. The agents had generally agreed to bargains which worked out at round about 10s. a week per man, which was in general higher than the bargains in adjoining mining leases. As the bargain was related partly to the price of lead, the lead market being fairly stable at a time when corn prices were increasing rapidly, this resulted in a steady lowering of the standard of living for the miners. Thomas Dodds, the agent for the North, realized this and suggested to the Court that he be allowed to make some other kind of bargain that would correct this. The Court, after considerable discussion, instructed all its agents to make the wages bargain independent of the current price of lead, but to make it in such a way that it would guarantee a fairly regular weekly wage to the miner, sufficient to maintain him in decency, to provide for education and recreation, and to keep him sufficiently fed whatever the price of food. To do this a monthly estimate of the cost of food was made, and the bargain rates adjusted to this. In July 1800, the bargain was giving about 10s. a week, and the readjustment made in August raised this to 12s. in response to the higher cost of bread. These measures were fairly satisfactory, and the agents report at intervals that there is less discontent and suffering on Alston Moor than in most other parts of the North. Towards 1815 and 1816 conditions again worsened, and this scheme of occasional purchases of grain began to fail. Mr. Stagg, the

* 1 bing—8 cwt.

Plate I Nent Head House, formerly called New House, the head offices and manager's house, built by the London Lead Company in 1753 and rebuilt in 1813.

Plate II Waterwheel and crushing rollers at the Killhope lead ore mill, Upper Weardale, in 1930.

Plate III Nent Head Smelt Mill.

Plate IV A later corner of Nent Head village. Rampgill Mine dressing floors behind on the left and the tip from Dowgang Level on the right.

FOOD IN THE FAMINE YEARS OF NINETEENTH CENTURY

new agent, advocated that the Company should take over entirely the supply of grain to the men, and again after some consideration, a scheme for this purpose was evolved. The Company authorized Stagg to purchase all the grain required, in Newcastle or Alston, and allowed him to issue to each miner a month's supply for his family and dependents, the cost being debited from his wage (the "bargains" were made quarterly, and wages paid monthly). In November 1816, the Court instructed Stagg that the corn was to be issued to the men "at a certain price, according to the Rate of Wages paid them", wheat was to be sold as near as possible to cost price, but rye could be sold at a loss of about 5s. per boll. In 1817 the agent reported the great advantage of this plan, and that the loss on the first year of its working was only about £100. 1,000 quarters of rye were bought the next year, and "we wish this to be supplied at the Market price, though it may entail loss". The insistence on market price reveals one of the greatest factors in the distress in the area, that is the very high charges made for transport of grain from Newcastle market, over the hills to the remote areas of Alston Moor and Westmorland. The Company's loss was largely on this cost of carriage and agents' charges, etc.

Apart from very condensed minutes and index items, the details of the scheme for supply of corn at this period are very scant; but, fortunately, the first few pages of a large MSS. book of surveyors' dialings and mine notes, made about 1816 to 1820, have been used by the Nent Head agent as a "journal", and among the notes of mine surveys are several entries that provide at least a skeleton picture of events. The following are the relevant entries:—

1817.

March 5. We have this day removed the Desk, Books, etc., from the Nent Head old Office, to the new one prepared at the New House,—and got a supply of Oat Meal into the other for the Workmen at which they seem very glad.

March 7. A supply of Oat Meal has this day been delivered to the Workmen, which is a most seasonable relief—And after all that can be done, on Acct. of the dearness of the times, they are many of them almost in a state of Starvation.

In addition to the dearness of food, the winter of 1816-17 had been one of unusual storms, and for months at a time it had been impossible to continue work on the open air washing floors, either because of excessive floods or because long continued frost had frozen up the dams and water wheels.

March 11. On account of Snow, our outside men are all idle which causes us a troublesome time, a part of them being extremely uneasy to have employment in the Mines.

March 14. This is almost the first day we have had this season, that has been calm. The Washers are become all at once exceeding clamourous to be set to wash, and I have been making a general looking through the Washing places, which are all in the most ruinous and wretched condition imaginable, and I consider it the best way (after dressing up a few parcels of odd ore that are in the way), to new model the Convenience altogether.

March 15. Spent the day at Alston purchasing Oat Meal etc. for the Workmen.

March 17. We have this day been taking the names of the Washers and are almost teazed to pieces by the Applications, by both Men and Women of all descriptions, the state of the place is very distressing after all that can be done. Numbers declare they cannot subsist at all without employment in Washing, and getting quit of the Women seems at present impossible.

March 18. We now have a number of hands put on at Water Races, Wheel Cases, Quarries, etc, and we are kept continually upon duty among them, and it is no easy matter to keep them all properly employed.

March 21. This has been a very busy day delivering Oat Meal to the Workmen. At the close of this days delivery (this being the last for the present month) it appears the consumption is about 72 Alston Bushels or 108 Bolls.

March 24. The whole of this day has been spent among the out door Men at the Water Races, etc., being good weather we have a number of that kind to attend to—I find this day that we have about 30 men out of employment, which together with a number of Washing Boys, makes the teasing almost intolerable.

April 2. Filling up the Advance list, which on account of the Meal, Rye, etc., is an extremely busy job and one of the most unpleasant I ever engage with.

April 3. Delivering Oat Meal and almost smothered with the crowd—at the end of each month, a considerable part of the population is almost on the brink of starvation.

THE CORN ASSOCIATION

May 26. This and the following Day was taken up in letting the Alston Moor Bargains and the remainder of the week wholly taken up in making out the Bargain list, Advance list, delivering Oat Meal to the Workmen, and assisting at making the Advances.

Further entries of days spent at Alston purchasing oatmeal, etc., occur for June and July, before the journal finishes. The frequent references to advances refers to part of the bargain system. In order to secure the miner against entire loss of wages for a period if a bargain does not produce at once, a monthly advance of wages was often allowed to the men, an adjustment or balance being struck at the end of the three months bargain period. Until 1820 this method of delivering corn was continued, but at the end of that year the Company gave each workman an advance of one month's wages, with a request that this money be used to initiate the scheme among the workmen themselves, the Company being guarantors of their solvency. This arrangement worked successfully until the recurrence of famine conditions in the "Hungry Forties". In 1841 the position had again become acute, and though the Company had repeatedly advanced wages to meet higher cost of food, etc., there was again widespread suffering through dearness of bread. The Court urged the miners to form their own Corn Association, and promised to give it aid " as circumstances arise ". This was done, and the Association soon reported considerable success. A similar Corn Association was formed at Middleton-in-Teesdale with equally good results.

In effect, these Corn Associations were actually pioneer Co-operative Societies. The workmen, through their own committee, using in the first case the advance of money (a month's wages) made by the Company, purchased their corn in bulk in the Newcastle market, and with the co-operation of the Company's excellent system of carriers were able to transport it to Nent Head or Garrigill at minimum cost. The mill at Tynebottom was handed over to their management, and everyone was able to get his corn ground there for no more than the cost of working. Until about 1860 the Associations were very active, with the fullest support of the Company, and in bad years with generous subscriptions from the Company funds. There were occasional grants of

£100 to the Corn Association, and a yearly grant of £25 towards the expenses of organization, with a larger grant of £150 in 1845 towards the cost of the Association building its own granary. The agents report that the general effect of the Associations was to create a closer bond between the men and the Company, and also to give the men a sense of responsibility in running their own concern. Along with other social amenities provided, it helped to keep Chartism away from the mining population.

Related in character to the Corn Association was the Ready Money Shop, which had been established at an early date in Nent Head, and later in Middleton. This was a shop built by the Company, and leased to a shopkeeper who was held by a bond not to allow any goods to leave the shop except for cash payment. The shop was in no way controlled by the Company except through the binding clauses of the lease, but at frequent periods the Company assisted the shop by arranging for the purchase of stores on a large scale in Newcastle, allowing the use of their transport system, and supplying a commodious and well-fitted warehouse, so that the shop could carry large stocks, and keep fairly stable prices. This was aimed mainly at the credit traders who would advance goods at ruinous prices, on credits to be cleared at the next month's wage payments. Through this system many of the miners lived constantly in debt, the whole of one month's wages being pledged in advance for goods supplied on credit. With the success of the Ready Money Shop, the credit traders practically disappeared, and the men had the advantage of choice of a very large stock of goods at very moderate price. The Company realized that the greatest advantage would be gained if the whole population of the district were sharers in the advantages, and from the beginning both the Corn Mill, the Ready Money Shop and the Corn Association, as also the schools, were open to all residents in Alston Moor and the various other districts of the Company's mines. This prevented the antagonism that might arise if the employees of one concern formed a favoured group in a general population that was suffering under adverse conditions. This policy was fully justified, and was in great part responsible for the tremendous respect in which the " Quaker Company " is still held in the district by farmers, miners, and all alike, though many of the families were never employed by it, and it is now fifty-five years since the Company left the area. They created an undying tradition of loyalty to, and care for, the whole district.

Notes to Chapter I

[1] Minute in 1728. "Whereas our Chief Agent in Flintshire Thos Barker hath in Severall of his Lettrs represented to us the Scarceity of Corn and the Hardships the poor Miners Smelters and others were under by the advanced price thereof and that if they were not Speedilly supplied he should be obliged to raise their Wages to allay their great Complaints and keep them Quiet being at the same time Sensible how difficult it will be for us to reduce their advanced Wages hereafter to prevent which Inconveniency we think it is for the Interest of the Company and will Redound much to their Reputation to send them a Supply of Corn from hence being much Cheaper than at their Markets.

"Therefor we desire the Treasurer that he will give orders for the hiring of a vessel abt 60 Tunns and for the buying about 400 Quarters of Corn vizt : 280 qrs of Barley 80 qrs of Wheat and 80 qrs of Oates for the relief of the Miners Smelters and others who are Imployed in our severall Workes there."

CHAPTER II

Workmen's Benefit Fund, and the Society of Miners of Alston Moor, 1755—The Medical Services of the Company—Annuities for Disablement—Accidents, Causes, etc. Plans of Mines.

FROM its formation in 1704, the Company had been careful for the miners' general health. During the nineteenth century much thought and money was spent on promoting miners' welfare and medical benefit societies, with the co-operation of the men. No organization, however, was proposed by the Company until about 1800, but during the eighteenth century the miners of Alston Moor banded themselves together in an association approximating to a Friendly Society, and this later was absorbed into the Company's welfare fund and schemes. The society was based on regular subscriptions, with graded benefits for ill health, accident, and death, and had a very comprehensive set of rules and orders, many of which are of special interest and some of rather humorous aspect.

ARTICLES, RULES, and ORDERS,

To be observed and kept by the Society of MINERS in ALDSTONE-MOOR in the County of Cumberland; whose Hands and Seals are hereunto set and subscribed the 31st of January, in the Year of our Lord, 1755.

Whereas it hath been an ancient Custom, in this Kingdom of Great-Britain, for divers Artists to meet together, and to unite themselves into Societies, to promote Amity and the true Christian Charity, and upon all just Occasions to assist each other. It is therefore agreed on as follows:—

Imprimis.

That the members of this Society shall have their meeting the first time on the 31st of January, 1755, and to continue their club every Friday six-weeks after, each member spending at every time twopence, and putting sixpence in the box: to meet at seven and part at ten.

II. That the landlord of the house shall be obliged to keep a good fire in the club-room in the winter season during the above mentioned hours or forfeit sixpence to the box.

III. That there shall be provided a box with three locks, one key to be kept by the landlord of the house, and the other two by the two stewards.

IV. That there shall be chosen two stewards out of this society, who shall serve six months, and afterwards to be chosen as they stand in the roll : that there shall be chosen six members out of this society, who, with the stewards, shall decide any dispute which may arise : and if the society think it not legal, it shall be put to the vote, by way of ballot, and shall be decided by a majority of votes.

V. That the stewards for the time being shall provide a feast, the first club day after Lammas, towards which every member shall pay sixpence, to be collected the club night before by the stewards : and upon the feast day, every member at his entrance into the club room, shall pay sixpence more to the stewards then in being : and upon any person's refusal, he or they shall forfeit sixpence to the box or be excluded this society, over and above the one shilling to be paid as aforesaid, and shall on the feast day be subject to these articles till ten at night, and be under the direction of four persons to be named by the stewards : which four persons shall preside in four companies, as the members of this society shall be divided by the stewards then in being, or forfeit sixpence to the box over and above the two sixpences, and the other forfeits mentioned to be paid on the feast day in this article, or be excluded this society ; and if either of the stewards send any victuals out of the club room on any feast day, such stewards, so offending, shall forfeit two shillings, and any other member one shilling.

VI. That the stewards chosen at the end of every six months, refusing to stand being fairly elected, shall forfeit two shillings and sixpence each, to be put into the box.

VII. That every member that entereth this society, betwixt the twenty-eighth day of March, 1754 and the twenty-eighth day of March, 1757, shall pay one shilling entrance, and eight pence for his club and box money ; and any other person that entereth this society, after the twenty-eighth day of March, 1757, shall pay two shillings and sixpence entrance, and eight pence for his club and box money, making in all three shillings and two pence.

VIII. Any member that calleth the stewards by any other name than Mr. Steward, during club hours, shall forfeit two pence ; and all forfeits due from any person offending shall be immediately paid, or else the person so offending shall be excluded.

IX. That no person shall be admitted into the society without a majority of votes, and none above thirty years of age ;

nor any person that hath any known ailment, either in mind or body.

X. That if any member, at the end of three years after he hath been a member, falls sick, lame, or infirm by age, so that he is rendered incapable of working, such member shall receive four shillings per week the first ten weeks; and if he lies more than ten weeks incapable of working, he shall receive two shillings and sixpence per week after.

XI. If any member die after he hath been a member three years, there shall be paid to his widow, executors, administrators, or assigns, three pounds; to which charge every surviving member shall contribute sixpence, next meeting after the interment, besides the sixpence for the six weeks meeting; and if any member refuses to pay the same, he or they so offending, shall be excluded.

XII. If it be proved that any member has followed business during his receiving money out of the box, upon any pretence of sickness or lameness, he shall be excluded this society: and he shall be sick or lame seven days before he shall receive such benefit from the box, not but that he shall be paid for that time when expired.

XIII. At the funeral of any member, the stewards and the six men chosen, or a man for them, shall meet at the club room at the time appointed, and shall spend their two pence, and accompany the stewards to the house of the deceased, and from thence to the place of interment, and back to the club room, or forfeit sixpence; and if any of them come disguised with liquor to any such funeral, he or they so offending shall forfeit one shilling, or be excluded, and they to pay at the next club day but fourpence towards the funeral charge, by reason of their attending.

XIV. That if any member disclose any business belonging to this society, he shall for every such offence forfeit the sum of five shillings, or be excluded.

XV. That if any member swears or curses during club hours, he shall forfeit two pence; or if he gives abusive language or occasions any quarrels, he shall forfeit one shilling to the box.

XVI. That if any person asketh for, or plays at cards, during club hours, he shall forfeit sixpence to be put in the box.

XVII. That no member shall call for drink or tobacco, during club hours, without the steward's leave, on forfeiture of two pence, to be put in the box; and if more drink is called for than the members' club money amounts to, the stewards shall pay it out of their own pockets.

XVIII. That if any member comes disguised with liquor into the club room, he shall forfeit two pence to be put into the box.

XIX. That every member shall be present at every meeting, or send his club and box money, otherwise forfeit twopence, besides his other forfeits ; if he is absent the second meeting, without sending his club and box money, and other forfeits, he shall forfeit four pence ; and if he is absent the third meeting, without sending his club and box money and his other forfeits, he shall be excluded this society.

XX. That whoever upbraids any member for receiving the benefit of the box, he or they offending shall forfeit sixpence to the box or be excluded.

XXI. That no member's wife shall enter the club room on any pretence, unless to bring her husband's money or forfeits, and then to depart immediately, on forfeiture of two pence, to be put into the box.

XXII. That if any member be in the country, and falls sick or lame, upon sending a certificate from the minister and church-wardens of the parish where he is sick or lame, he shall receive the benefit of the box.

XXIII. No member or members that shall at any time be excluded this society, shall have any right to draw anything out of this box, without entering as new members.

XXIV. That no member shall attempt the breaking up of this box or this society, unless the members be reduced to three, on forfeiture of one shilling to the box ; so that if there be four, this society shall continue ; and when less, the remaining number may open the box, and divide the money in equal shares.

XXV. That the stewards are obliged to be in the club room half an hour after the commencement of the club hour, or send their key, on forfeiture of sixpence to the box ; and that every other member shall be in the club room at eight o'clock or forfeit two pence, to be put into the box ; unless a lawful reason be shown, that meeting or the next.

XXVI. That if any member shall privately design or promote the breaking up of the box, the member hearing the same, and not discovering it, shall immediately be excluded.

XXVII. That all forfeitures whatsoever shall be paid into the box ; and if any member refuses to pay the same he shall be immediately excluded.

XXVIII. If any member enlists himself into his Majesty's service, either by sea or land, as a volunteer ; if he come home safe from wounds or lameness, for paying up his club money, box money, and other forfeits, from the time he enlisted, he shall be admitted into this society again.

XXIX. That no money shall be taken out of the box on any account whatsoever, without an order signed by the stewards and the majority of the six, for the time being ; and that the said six members chosen at the end of every six months by the stewards for the time being, shall attend the stewards at the club room, on a proper summons from the beadle, if they are in town, or forfeit sixpence, to be put into the box ; and if either of the stewards, or any of the six as above, disclose any business directly or indirectly, that shall be transacted at such their meeting or meetings, to any of the other members, or to any person of this society, he or they shall, for every such offence, forfeit the sum of five shillings or be excluded.

XXX. That no member who hath been afflicted with any distemper from his infancy, or hath contracted one by a wicked and debauched way of living ; or if it be proved that he got his misfortune by quarrelling, drunkenness, wrestling, etc., he shall not receive any benefit from the box for any such lameness or mischance.

XXXI. That if any member urge or propose any wager, or undervalue any member in his employment, he shall forfeit sixpence.

XXXII. That if any member, after he hath been a member three years, be entitled, by sickness or death, by himself or assigns, to any benefit from the box, and shall legally demand the same, and be refused, shewing that he is legally entitled, he shall prosecute the stewards for the time being for the same.

XXXIII. That if any member divulge or discover any conversation directly or indirectly, that shall pass during club hours, he shall forfeit two shillings and sixpence, or be immediately excluded.

XXXIV. That at all meetings, the stewards for the time being, shall have power to command silence ; and any member refusing to obey the same, shall forfeit twopence ; and if any member having anything to offer relative to this society, he shall speak, and shall get up and address himself to the stewards, who having commanded silence, he shall speak his mind, and sit down in his place again ; and then any other member having anything to offer for or against anything that hath been spoken, shall likewise address himself to the stewards, who having commanded silence, and having spoken and having done, he likewise shall sit down in his place. Only one shall be allowed to speak at a time, till the debate is ended, and then the stewards shall put it to a vote.

XXXV. If any member of this society disguises himself in liquor on the Sabbath day, commonly called Sunday, he shall for every such offence forfeit sixpence.

XXXVI. That whatever house this box shall be lodged in, the landlord, master, or mistress of the said house, shall give good security for the box, money, bonds, notes, and other papers, and other things of value deposited in the said box ; and that the said landlord, master, mistress, etc., of the said house, shall give a promissory note to the stewards for the time being, for all the money that is in the box, every six weeks, if required.

XXXVII. That if any member conceal a fraud, committed by any drawing member, he shall forfeit five shillings, but if any member be charged with any felonious matter, he shall be excluded this society, until he shall be lawfully acquitted of the same, and clearly discharged by law.

XXXVIII. That at all six weeks meetings, which is a time for all members to be there present, if it is thought fit, by the majority of the society, to make new orders, they shall be entered in a book for that purpose, and shall be in as much force as any of the foregoing orders, provided they do not lessen any of the articles contained therein.

XXXIX. That if any debate shall arise in the society, that no article herein can fully determine, it shall be determined by a majority of votes, and then only one person shall be allowed to speak at a time.

XL. No person of a bad character, or who goes under the name of an idle, debauched person, shall be admitted into this society.

XLI. That all persons who have a mind to enter into this society shall give notice of it to the stewards six weeks before they shall be admitted, and the stewards shall give the report to the society ; and if any member know any ailment, infirmity, or distemper, with that person, or if he be a loose, debauched, idle person, such member shall make his report to the stewards, at or before the next club night, of his ailments ; and if he be fit to be a brother, and clear of such ailments, he shall be admitted.

XLII. That every member shall clear off his arrears at the change of the stewards, at the end of every six months, or forfeit sixpence.

XLIII. It is further agreed that the box and society shall be continued and kept at the house of MICHAEL WALTON, in Aldstone, if he conforms to the aforesaid articles and orders.

XLIV. That every member of this society shall have a printed copy of these articles, at his own expense, that he may be made sensible of everything contained herein.

This Society of Miners of Aldstone Moor was one of the earliest of the Friendly Societies that sprang up during the Industrial Revolution, but was by no means unique. Curwen, the Cumberland colliery owner, formed a benefit fund in 1786, at his collieries at Workington and Harrington, to which his employees were compelled to pay 6d. per week, the employer paying one-third of the sum thus subscribed. The fund was managed by a committee of workmen chosen by themselves, but was under the very strict supervision of the employer. In 1816 Curwen proposed in Parliament a universal scheme on these lines, as a substitute for the Poor Law. Many societies like that of Alston Moor were organized solely by the workers, and independent of the employers, but in the famine and strike years 1816-19 these were viewed with the gravest suspicion by many magistrates as disguised forms of illegal workmen's combinations, and it was maintained that in some cases the " box " had been broken up to provide " strike funds ". In 1819 an Act of Parliament was passed to give some control over the Friendly Societies, but long before that time the Alston society had been re-organized into the Company's Workmen's Fund, with the Company the largest subscriber to it.

The Society of Miners was active throughout the latter part of the century, but as its liabilities increased the Company were asked to come to its aid on various occasions, and several grants were made and entered in the Company accounts as donations to the Workmen's Fund. In 1813 the association was reorganized financially as the Workmen's Fund, with a committee of workmen still entirely in charge of it. The Company accepted a measure of responsibility by guaranteeing its funds and keeping it solvent by annual grants, based on the particular needs of each year. From 1827 to 1867 under the new arrangement the Company subscribed a total of £12,260 to the Fund, in addition to wiping off an adverse balance at the beginning of the period, of £1,380. By 1840 the Fund was subscribed to by nearly all the miners, and at the end of that year, after an investigation of its affairs by an actuary, the Workmen's Fund was found to be entirely solvent without the Company's subscription. The subscriptions, none the less, were continued, and in 1860 it had a large balance in hand, and requested leave of the Court to increase sick benefit payments and old age allowances, a permission most gladly given.

In the early years of the Fund the committee paid their own Medical Officer, hence the occasional appearance of the instruction to the doctor " to get men well by early attention, and so save the Fund ". In 1827 the Company decided, for many reasons, to take over the entire responsibility of medical attention for the miners, and proceeded to appoint its own surgeons and assistants as Company officers, at first at Nent Head and Middleton-in-Teesdale, but later at other districts under their charge. These medical men were instructed to attend *all* workpeople and their families, whether they subscribed to the Fund or not. The Nent Head surgeon was provided with a house rent free in the village, and had a salary of £150, raised in 1864 to £250, with an allowance for horse, etc. In Middleton the salary was £300, but the doctor had to attend not only the whole of Teesdale and Lunehead, but also Weardale. He was allowed £70 for an assistant, and later two other assistants were appointed to be resident in outlying districts in Westmorland and North Yorkshire, with allowances of £60 and houses. The total cost of the medical services, calculated for a panel of over 1,650 families scattered over nearly 1,000 square miles of mountainous country, was, for the first half of the nineteenth century, just less than 10s. per family per year, and several visiting medical inspectors commented on the excellence and efficiency of the service.

The Company laid down very strict rules for the guidance of the conduct of their doctors, and for the conduct of the funds, and in 1829 decided to codify all their various rules, and supply them in the contract of appointment. The rules are as follows :—

RULES AND REGULATIONS
to be observed by the medical gentlemen in the employment of
the LEAD COMPANY.

To Mr..........................
Sir,
You having been appointed Medical Attendant to the Workmen in the employment of the Governor and Company, I am directed by the Court of Directors to call your attention to the following instructions.
I am, Sir,
your obedient servant,
Middleton House. 18....

You are to attend upon all the afflicted members and their families residing within your district, as often as the nature of the complaint may require, and supply them with and send them such medicine, etc., as the nature of their afflictions require ; and in case of accident or sudden dangerous illness, you must visit, or procure a person, properly qualified, to visit any such member, by night or by day, *with all convenient speed*, and render all the assistance you, or such medical practitioner is capable of rendering. And you shall hold your office so long as you discharge the duties, and perform the engagements to the Company with fidelity, honour, and to the satisfaction of the Court.

For those men who are *Members of the Workmen's Fund* you must sign the Certificate which the afflicted member is to send, each month, for his money, every time you visit him ; and it is essentially necessary, for the information and guidance of the Committee, that you do always, at your first visit, write the nature of the member's complaint on his sickness paper ; and on the back thereof, the state of the member's health upon each subsequent visit, the date of which is to be inserted.

You are to visit personally, at their own homes, the sick members, immediately you are required to do so, as it will occur that the progress of fever may be arrested, and its otherwise regular course prevented by timely assistance.

And in internal inflammation, so prevalent among the working classes, the important period of a few hours being lost for blistering or bleeding, fatal consequences ensue, rendering all future attempts at remedying fruitless.

In case of accident, also, the prompt assistance of a medical gentleman will, of course, frequently prevent after mischiefs and tedious complaints.

You are never to require members of the sick fund to attend at your residence, for advice, nor the sickness paper to be brought there for signature ; and to be particular that *all medicines*, etc., *furnished to them, are carefully labelled*.

(Those persons only who do not declare on the fund for the sick relief, or, if not members of the fund, whose diseases are trivial, to be required to wait on the medical gentlemen for medicine or advice.)

You must impress on the sick members the proper regimen to be observed for their complaints ; and when it may be conducive to their health, you must prescribe, distinctly, *the hours of the day* during which it will be really beneficial for them to take the air.

And in your visits and intercourse with the members and their families, you must bear in mind that not only prompt personal attendance, but *the highest degree of courtesy and kindness of manner* is requisite towards them, they being, generally, more susceptible to slights than persons of more liberal education, and of the higher walks of life.

Lastly, the Court wish to impress upon you the consequences which must arise, if members (who are not apt to declare on the

THE MEDICAL SERVICES OF THE COMPANY

sick fund too early, but rather otherwise), be slightingly attended to, or a trifling medicine sent them by an assistant, or from neglect to label medicines with the proper directions, and not impressing on sick members the best regimen to be observed, etc.,—*diseases will be protracted, or disorders confirmed, to the danger of life*,—to the serious injury of the workmen's fund,—*and protracted attendance of the medical gentlemen themselves.*
London. 26th March, 1829.

In spite of the greatest care, and the very good housing conditions, there were a few epidemics in the area, though all were reported as being less serious in their losses by death within the Company's areas than in the surrounding districts. Typhus appeared in Stanhope and Middleton-in-Teesdale districts about February 1818, and the Court at once ordered that " Wine and whatever else may contribute to their restoration and comfort " be supplied at once and at the Company's cost to *all* sufferers. Dr. McWhirter, Physician to the Newcastle Fever Hospital, was called in by the Court, a little later, to report on the epidemic and the measures taken to fight it, and he was pleased to congratulate the Company on their very efficient measures. Later, in November of the same year, he reported that " the supply of wine and other comforts have confessedly saved the lives of many of the workmen and their families ". At the end of the year, the Court made Dr. McWhirter a present of £50 as a token of esteem for his help and friendliness during a difficult time, this being in addition to his professional fees. The epidemic by prompt measures was confined to a fairly limited area, and hardly spread to Nent Head or into the upper reaches of Teesdale. All clothes and bedding of the fever patients was ordered to be destroyed by fire, and replaced by new ones, after recovery, and it is reported that this measure did much to keep the fever in check and to prevent its recurrence. There was a slight second epidemic of typhus in 1830.

In 1837 a form of influenza spread rapidly among the workpeople, but was eventually got under control and eliminated. Scarlet fever and a small outbreak of typhoid fever was experienced in 1847, but again it was perhaps very significant that the disorder was almost entirely limited to the villages of Stanhope in Weardale, and to the various hamlets in Teesdale, in the planning and building of which the Company had little or no part. In the Company villages of Nent Head, Hilton, Murton, etc., the fevers were almost unknown.

The first symptoms of cholera appeared in the North on April 17th, 1849, and on April 20th the Court ordered its agents and managers to take all possible precautions to prevent the spread of this disease amongst their workmen. The disease did spread, however, in spite of all preventive measures, but was, fortunately, never severe within the Company's areas. The Court decided almost at once to order the overhaul and redesign of most of the water supplies on their properties, and very considerable sums were spent on building reservoirs out of reach of all contamination and in piping supplies to all houses and cottages both at Nent Head and at Middleton-in-Teesdale, and a year or so later at Hilton, Dufton, Garrigill and Stanhope. The effect of the good water supply was soon apparent in improved health among the workmen and cleanliness in the cottages. At Nent Head a public bath house was added in the village. In 1861, Dr. Headlam Greenhow, the Government Inspector of Health, sent a very warmly worded testimony to the Court in favour of the Company's health regulations for the benefit of their workpeople, and in 1863 Dr. Peacock, another Government Inspector, wrote the Court congratulating them on the splendid record of health among their workmen in the Teesdale districts he had just inspected. It is clear from numerous minutes and reports that the agents for the North were able, time after time, to assure the Court that the general health of the workpeople was vastly better as a result of their regulations and services, and that loss of time and money by sickness was now reduced to a small figure, the consequent saving offsetting many times the cost of the health services.

In 1834 the Workmen's Fund is described as follows :—

Each man pays 30/- a year to a general fund, and receives therefrom during sickness or inability to work, 8s. per week for six weeks, and afterwards 6s. per week as long as he needs it and remains incapable of following his employment. At 65 years of age each miner is allowed 5s. per week for life. The Company at their own expense provide medical assistance in addition to the above, not only for the men themselves, but in every case that it is needed by their wives and families.

ANNUITIES FOR DISABLEMENT

The Workmen's Fund thus made provision for weekly payments to men disabled by age from continuing their work, but the scheme in no way served as a pensions fund for the officials and office workers. The Court never saw its way to forming such a pension scheme, but from its very inception, the Company adopted the practice of providing for its officials and senior clerks, by annuities granted at the retirement of the individual, and based upon his position and service. This seems to have been very thorough, and there is no evidence that anyone was left out even to the extent of the Company providing small annuities for widows and dependants of servants who died while in their employ. A few examples will perhaps serve to indicate the scale of these payments :—

		£
1816	John Smith, Mill agent	50 per ann.
1824	Widow of Joshua Stagg, agent	50
	John Pinkney, Mine agent and donation of £21 for education of his children.	20
1826	Widow of Matth. Powell, mill agent	20
1835	Widow of John Readshaw £20 continued to his children until 21, should she marry again.	
1836	Middleton Hewitson, agent	100
1845	John Millican, agent, Nent Head	200

Other annuities fall into two or three definite groups, the agents for the North vary, £100, £120, £200, £250, and the largest, £500, to Robert Stagg, general agent, in 1851, which he drew for thirteen years. He had been an agent of the Company since 1809, and was responsible for carrying out many of the reforms dealt with in these chapters. The Company on many occasions made him presents to express their appreciation of his careful stewardship, and as early as 1817 proposed to him the grant of an annuity. In that year his salary was increased to £1,000 per annum, and the Court granted him an annuity of £300 for fourteen years certain, to accumulate for the benefit of his family. The £300 a year was invested in the hands of Trustees, " with the unanimous approbation of the Court, for his constant and strenuous exertions for the promotion of the interests of the Company ". Annuities of £30 were regularly granted to various workmen who were outside the provisions of the Fund, such as to woodmen on the estates, to the gardeners at Middleton, and to the mill agents, while £20 per annum was granted generally to the widows of such employees, and to the widows of the smaller mill agents at Hilton, Dufton, Stanhope, etc.

In addition, and often as a supplement to annuities, the Company invariably made a gratuity to a retiring employee who was not provided for by the fund, gratuities being generally £20, £30, £50 or £100. In addition there was also a system of gratuities for special services. Again there was no ruling and no special scale, but it was an old custom of the Court, on report to it by an agent of a particular piece of work carried through by one person, to make a gratuity to that person. Again, the general sum was something from 20 to 50 guineas. The kind of work for which these presents were given would now rank as overtime jobs—for extra time spent in completing a survey of a mine—extra work in the remodelling of a mill—trouble in renewing or extending some leases—for improvement in a way of working, etc.; and along with these, very numerous gratuities given to meet " extra cost due to illness "—or a period at the seaside to recover health, etc. It is abundantly clear from the scores and scores of such entries in the minutes, that the Court was kept in close touch with the actual individuals employed by them, and cherished a keen sense of personal responsibility. The contact was kept through the agents, who reported to all meetings of the Court, and attended frequently, the agent for each district keeping in touch with the men by personal inspection of all mines and works, and regular contact with the under agents and men's deputations. In spite of its large size, the Company kept something of a family contact with all its workpeople and their families.

To meet the special cases of accident and impaired health through special conditions (lead poisoning, etc.), the Court in 1810 established a fund for maimed and decayed workmen, and from this made quarterly grants, or in case of permanent disablement gave annuities. As the Workmen's Fund flourished towards the middle of the century, the accidents were transferred to it, and the accident fund was added to the sick fund.

ACCIDENTS, CAUSES, ETC. PLANS OF MINES

The accident record of the Company was, in comparison with general figures for the industry, very low, and this was largely due to the fact that in each district mine captains were appointed, who were to be responsible, among other things, for the safety of all working places. In addition, all the mines were regularly inspected not only by the overmen of the district, but by the agents from all other districts. In the course of the first sixty-five years of the nineteenth century, only twenty-one men were killed in the mines, with nearly 1,000 men employed. The causes of each accident were reported to the Court, and a special report called for to indicate how such an accident could be prevented for the future, and whether or not any fresh modification of regulations was needed. The following list will indicate the nature of the risks run in the work, and the comments of the Court may also prove of some interest :—

1829   John Millican, District agent, crushed by falling in of a mine.

1830   Two men killed, by falling in of a mine, one in Alston Moor & one in Teesdale, and one man seriously injured at the same time.

1833   John Brown, miner, killed by the falling in of a rock, in Lodgesyke mine.
A man killed in Flakebrigg Mine, by falling in of a rock, his 5 partners narrowly escaped.

1836   Thomas Tatters, drowned in Cappelcleugh mine—his son was with him—miraculously saved.
Robinson, a boy, crushed to death by a waggon, in Cappelcleugh mine.

1844   John Nixon, drowned in Mannergill Mine by the irruption of water from the old man's workings.

1848   William Wallace killed Stanhope Burn Mine, Thomas Little killed Browngill Low Level, both by falling in of the roof.

1852   John Allinson, killed, Ashgill Head Mine Level, contrary to regulation, riding in the waggon.

1855   Joseph Wallace, a labourer, killed in Smallcleugh Mine—carelessness on own part.
another labourer injured in the head by a shot, at Little Eggleshope mine, not attending to rules.

1856 Robinson, 18 years old, crushed to death in Coldberry Mill.
1857 John Wilkinson, killed in Handsom Mea mine, roof fell in.
1858 a washer boy drowned while bathing in Little Eggleshope Reservoir.
1859 John Robinson 23½ years, killed in Cappelcleugh Low level, by fall of a stone, result of his own carelessness.
1861 Thomas Liverick killed in Middlecleugh mine, falling in of roof.
1863 Collinson a miner, accidentally killed in Cornish Hush mine.

Of smaller accidents, there are a few cases of injury to sight due to neglect of the regulations for using blasting powder, and on several occasions the Court had to warn the men that the only accidents other than fall of roof were almost entirely due to neglect of regulations made for their own safety. It is abundantly clear that in the above list, the major cause of accidents is the falling in of roof. This is still responsible for the great majority of mine accidents, and cannot be foreseen. The only remedy, and that not an infallible one, is most careful propping, and time after time the Court emphasize that there must be no stint of timber to the mines. Their own plantations provided abundantly for all that could be demanded, and the result of that generous policy is seen in the relatively very low death rate. The list of accidents is also illuminating in the remarkably small number of other accidents than those from roof trouble. It is clear that the Company through its excellent organization of the miners had secured almost the maximum possible safety of working. The accident at Mannergill, where a man was drowned by inrush of water, and a similar accident at Cappelcleugh, emphasize what is still one of the most dreaded accidents in mining, that of " holing through " into long-abandoned workings (universally referred to as " the old man's works ", the old man being the old time miner), which are almost always " watered up ", that is, entirely filled with water, often under considerable head or pressure. The only possible safeguard against this danger is intimate and reliable knowledge of exactly where " the old man " worked. This can only be had if reliable plans of

ACCIDENTS, CAUSES, ETC. PLANS OF MINES

workings are kept, and at an early date* the Company employed surveyors, and established a system of plan recording that called forth the admiration of the Greenwich Hospital inspectors in 1821, who particularly commented on the great value for the future of the splendid plans the Company were keeping not only of all present workings, but also of all old workings they could locate. One of the most valuable of the Company manuscripts, now in the Institute of Mining Engineers at Newcastle-on-Tyne, is a volume of over 100 carefully-drawn and large-scale plans of their mines in Alston Moor and Teesdale.

* 1815. Plans and sections of Mines, first completed at Stanhope.
 1816. Do. for Alston Moor with details of all workings.
 1818. Report to Court of great advantages of plans and record of workings of every mine.
 1822. Court complimented by inspectors on the admirable practical execution of their plans and sections.
 1824. Plans not to be inspected by strangers.
 1844. Proposed Act of Parliament for registering plans to be opposed.
 1859. Plans and drawings of slag hearths, etc., to be presented to Museum of Practical Geology (Geological Survey), London, etc., etc.

CHAPTER III

Education of the Workmen's Children—The Company's Day and Sunday Schools—Libraries and Lectures, Reading Rooms, etc.— Recreational Provisions—Training of Overmen, and Mines Council.

IT is natural in the records of a company such as this we are studying, to expect a prominent place to be given to educational work, and so far as the nineteenth century is concerned, the expectation is fully justified. In the earlier periods of the Company, references to educational activities are only few, and are scattered incidentally among the minutes of purely business transactions, so that only a very incomplete and sketchy picture can be presented, until more detailed material is discovered. There are occasional minutes which indicate that the managers were allowed to use the offices for small classes much in the nature of evening schools, where at least some of the boys and men in the Company's employ could be taught and given a little special training to make them more suitable for positions of responsibility in the offices and about the works. Many of the men were helped to learn to read and write, and also a large amount of indirect work was carried on through the Friends' Meetings established near all the Company's mining centres. We learn from Story's Journal, that even in the early years of the eighteenth century he was a frequent visitor to the northern districts, where he had meetings with the miners which were held both in the Nent valley and in Allendale.

When the Nent Head estate was developed and the new village created, the school was held in the Company's office, with a proper schoolmaster to take care of the miners' children, the schoolmaster probably being paid by the children's school pence. At the same time the Company established Sunday schools again to be held in their office buildings. For education other than this, the Company subscribed to the old Charity schools at Alston and Garrigill, but as most of the social work was put under the supervision of special committees for local reports, etc., and the minute books of the committees have all been destroyed, we are left only with slender references.

In 1808 the British and Foreign School Society had been formed, to create schools on the Lancasterian system, and in 1813, Robert Owen, in his new schools at New Lanark, was assisted by several Friends, notably by William Allen; the numerous Friends connected with the management of the Company, and on its Court, must have been fairly familiar with these experiments, and in a right frame of mind to encourage similar work in their own areas. In 1816 they gave generous subscriptions to extend their Sunday schools at Nent Head, Garrigill, and Middleton, and began to discuss the possibility of more regular day schools. Their agent in the north, Joseph Stagg, was a great enthusiast for the idea, and presented a scheme to the Court in 1817 by which the Company were to build their own schools, not under either the Lancaster or Bell systems, but under their own direction and supervision. In February 1818, the building of two schools was commenced, one at Nent Head and one at Middleton,* each to accomodate 200 children. It was decided by the Court to make it a condition of employment by the Company, that a miner's children should attend the school regularly, as well as attending Sunday school and a place of worship each week.

Boys were to attend the schools from the age of six years to twelve years, and girls from six years to fourteen years. As the leases held by the Company in Weardale were all within the lands held by the Bishop of Durham, the Court instructed its agents to discuss with him the necessity or desirability of a school in Weardale, and the Bishop agreed first to build a school, then to " place the schools on such a footing as most agreeable to the Court's views ". With this concession the Court expressed themselves as being very pleased, and agreed thereupon to give £400 towards the school to be erected at Stanhope in Weardale. This

---

* Mackenzie writing in 1835 gives some account of Middleton-in-Teesdale.

" The *Governors' School* was erected by the London Lead Company. Its dimensions are 20 yards by 12, and in winter it is warmed by stoves. The average number of scholars, boys and girls, is about 150, each of whom pays 1s. per quarter, orphans and children of widows excepted. The system of education is nearly similar to that used in the National Schools. A Sunday school is held in this building which is attended by about 250 scholars.

" The *Company's Library*, containing several hundred volumes, is kept in their offices, and is free to their workmen; but other persons pay 1s. per quarter each."

was done, and although practically all the children at the school were of parents in the Company's employ, the Court asked the Bishop to retain oversight and to appoint the master. Nent Head school was opened about the middle of 1819, and Middleton school opened with 155 children, 31st of May the same year. The Court and the agent, J. Stagg, were very much afraid of giving the schools a denominational flavour, so they decided that no books should be used in them, except the Scriptures and such as are used by all denominations—no catechism was to be taught nor any tenets peculiar to one church. An objection to attendance at the schools on " religious " grounds was to be accepted by the Company, and in the Weardale school an exemption was obtained for all miners' children, from the 20th rule making attendance at the Church of England compulsory. As soon as the schools at Nent Head and Middleton were well established, the Court turned to other and smaller areas such as Dufton, Hilton, and Lunedale (Harwood Forest) where the number of miners was not enough at first to support a school. In those areas, the Company subscribed to small parish or charity schools, and arranged for the miners' children to attend them at the same rate as at the Company's schools, the Company to pay the difference, as the school pence at the Company's schools were much lower than at any others. Smaller schools supported in this way during the earlier years, and in most cases either rebuilt or replaced by the Company later, were Ashgill, Carlebeck, Eggleston, Garrigill, Harewood, Holwick, Knock, Lunehead, Milburn, Mickleton, Newbiggin, Tynehead, Dufton and Gaunless, in all of which areas the Company had mines.

A set of rules and regulations was drawn up for the regulation of the schools, and is worthy of special study, when its date, 1819, is remembered.

REGULATIONS
of the
LEAD COMPANY'S SCHOOLS

WEEK-DAY SCHOOLS

1.—That the School Room be kept in order, and the Fire, Books, and Stationery be provided at the Expense of the Company.

The Parents of the Company's Workmen's Children taught at the School shall contribute one Shilling per Quarter for each child. And other parties shall be charged after the rate of Two Shillings and Sixpence per Quarter.

2.—That the School shall be opened with singing and prayer; and the Teaching be carried on not less than six hours each day, for five days in the week.

3.—That the Sacred Scriptures, in the authorised version, or extracts therefrom shall be read and taught in the School.

4.—That no Catechism, peculiar to any religious denomination shall be used in the School, nor any peculiar tenets of any religious sect inculcated on the Scholars.

5.—All Children belonging to the Lead Company's Workmen, and the Widows of deceased Workmen, shall be required to enter the Company's Week-Day School at Six Years of age (and earlier if the parents think fit). The Boys to attend from Six to Twelve years of age; and the Girls from Six to Fourteen years of age, if they so long remain under the paternal roof.

6.—Every Parent is required, on sending his or her child to School, to furnish the Teacher, in writing, with the date of the Child's birth.

7.—If Parents neglect to send their Children to School at Six years of age, or if, after entering School, the Children are at any time absent therefrom, they shall not be at liberty to quit School at the period above named, nor until they have completed the required time of attendance, viz. Six years in case of a Boy, and Eight years in case of a Girl.

8.—That every Child attending the Company's Week-Day School shall be required to attend twice every Sabbath such place of religious worship as his or her parents may think proper.

9.—No Child must be absent from School on any pretence whatever, unless he or she be sick, or have obtained leave from the Superintendent. If a Child be sick, the Parent, with the Child, are positively required to apply to the Company's Surgeon; who having seen the Child, will certify whether he or she be unable to attend School; and the like certificate must be produced whenever afterwards the Teacher may think proper.

10.—No Boy will be admissible to the Company's Works who cannot produce a certificate from the Company's Teacher, stating that he has complied with the above regulations, and that he has been of good behaviour, industrious, and has entered or is qualified to enter the Sabbath School.

Sabbath Schools

1.—That every child attending the Company's Week-Day School, shall, when required, attend the Sabbath School taught in the Company's School Room, on the Sabbath morning ; and, twice on the Sabbath day, such place of religious worship as his or her parents may think proper.

2.—Every child must be present at the hour fixed for the opening of the school, and must come prepared with such portions of the Catechism, Bible lesson, etc., as may have been previously appointed by the Superintendent or Teacher, and must conform to all the School regulations.

3.—That the Sacred Scriptures, in the Authorised Version, or Extracts therefrom, shall be read and taught in the School.

4.—That no Catechism peculiar to any religious denomination shall be used in the School, nor any peculiar Tenets of any religious Sect inculcated on the Scholars.

5.—A Certificate from the Sunday School Superintendent must be produced by every Boy applying to go to the Mine, or any of the Company's Works, certifying that he has been regular in his attendance at School, and place of religious worship, and that he has been industrious, and of good behaviour ; if the Superintendent cannot give him such required certificate, such Boy must attend the Week-Day School, till the Teacher thereof can give him a good character.

6.—Boys on attaining the age for working regularly underground will not be admitted unless they have passed their Bible examination, or can produce a certificate from the Sunday School Superintendent, giving a sufficient reason for their not having passed such examination, and stating that their conduct is correct, that they are industrious, and are making suitable progress.

7.—Any Boy absenting himself from School, or place of religious worship, or not conforming to the School regulations, or being guilty of any disorderly practices on the Sabbath, will subject himself to dismissal from the Company's works.

8.—Every Child of the Company's Workmen will be presented with a Bible, on the production of a certificate from the Company's School Inspector, that such Child has passed a satisfactory Bible Examination prior to leaving the Sabbath School at which such Child may have received instruction.

Exemptions Applicable to Both Schools

1.—In cases where the Company's Workmen reside at such a distance from the Company's Schools as may prevent the Children attending thereat, in this instance as respects the Week-Day

School, the Company contribute two shillings per quarter towards the education of each child taught at such school; provided the Company's School Inspector, on Examination, certify that the Child is being efficiently taught.

2.—In case wherein any of the Company's Workmen shall declare in writing, that they object, upon religious principles, to their Children being educated in the Company's Schools.

3.—In either of the said cases, the workmen will be required to send their Children to some other School for the full period named in the rules of the Company's Schools.

Provided that a Journal of the attendance, progress, and behaviour of such Children be furnished quarterly to the Company's Agent; also a certificate of their regular attendance at some place of religious worship.

4.—Boys educated as above, upon applying for work, will be required to produce certificates similar to those required from Boys educated in the Company's schools; such certificates being counter-signed by the Company's School Inspector, as regards the secular attainments of the Boy.

Along with the Regulations it is perhaps of special interest to have the first list of books ordered and supplied to the Nent Head School :—

Bought of Francis & John Rivington,
Booksellers,
No. 62, St. Paul's Church Yard,
and No. 3, Waterloo Place, Pall Mall.
The Governors of the Lead Company, Jan. 13th, 1819.
    50 sets Central School Cards.
    200 Central School Books No. 2.
    100 Sermon on the Mount & Parables.
    100 Miracles and Discourses.
    100 History of Our Saviour.
    100 Ostervalds Abridgment.
    100 Broken Catechism.
    100 Chief Truths.
    50 Trimmer's New Testament.
    50   do.   Old   do.
All these are now published by the Society for promoting Xn knowledge.

In looking over the rules it will be seen that they include for all children, far more than the provisions which the " Health and Morals of Apprentices Act " of 1802 had secured to the small class of bound apprentices, and that in fact, these regulations of 1818 include all and more than all the educational provisions of the Mining Act of 1860 which provided that no boy of ten to twelve years of age should be employed underground without a certificate from a competent schoolmaster that he could read and write or, failing that, that he was to attend school three hours a day, two days a week. What was secured for ten to twelve-year-olds in 1860 was already granted by the Company to all in 1818, and further, the school leaving age was already higher by two years, no boy being allowed to leave school before twelve. The Government Act of 1875 introduced " class subjects " such as geography, history and needlework to the elementary school curriculum, but needlework at least had been taught since 1818 in the Lead Company's schools. A needlework mistress was appointed at Nent Head and at Middleton in 1820, and a little later another was appointed for the smaller outlying schools. The appointment of a " schools inspector " ensured a high standard in all the Company's schools, and also in the many other schools to which the Company subscribed, and to which exempted miners' children were allowed to go (see Rule 1 of exemptions, quoted above). In 1840 the appointment was expanded and, in addition to school inspector, the official was to be school examiner, to hold an examination in all subjects, every quarter, in all schools. The Brougham Committee, sitting in 1818 and reporting on proposals for elementary schools, ruled that the salary of a master should not exceed £24 per annum, but the same year the Company appointed their own masters at Nent Head and Middleton, at £90 with a bonus of £10, and shortly after the bonus was confirmed as part of the fixed salary of £100—a very striking comment on the Brougham report.

In 1820 the miners of all districts sent a deputation to the Court to record " their gratitude for the Company's many acts of kindness and particularly for the establishment of schools ". Robert Stagg, who had prepared and presented the schemes for the regular Company schools to the Court, wrote after the opening of the Nent Head and Middleton schools in 1819 :—

> I cannot quit this subject without again repeating my thanks for the readiness with which my recommendation to establish

schools, was met by the Court ; and for the high gratification I have this day enjoyed in witnessing the commencement of an institution which will insure to the whole of the population a respectable education, and will I trust, lay the foundation for a radical and general improvement in the moral and religious habits of the rising generation ; and which can hardly fail eventually to prove beneficial to the Company, by training up more active and intelligent practical Agents, and by giving more orderly and correct habits to the workmen at large.

Again in 1847, Robert Stagg writes to the Court :—

Upwards of a quarter of a century has by now tested the soundness of the Principles adopted and the great value of these establishments, to the influence of which may mainly be attributed the total absence of rebellions and insubordinations of every kind ; and that chartism—radicalism—and every other abomination have for so very many years been strangers to the concern—and there does not exist today in the whole kingdom, a more orderly, industrious and contented body of workmen.

While we smile at the " abominations of chartism ", etc., we can still appreciate this great testimony to the value of kindly consideration and thought for the welfare of both workpeople and children.

The schools reflect the spirit of the times in their continual insistence on the religious and moral training as their prime duty, but in the attempt to carry out this idea the Company before long came into disagreement and conflict with the Bishop of Durham. At first, the masters appointed to the Company's schools were required to be members of the Church of England, as a guarantee of good character and respectability, and also to avoid the appearance of sectarianism. In 1849 the Bishop complained to the Court because they had appointed, in 1835, a new master who was a Presbyterian. The Bishop insisted that all the Company's schools were founded as Church schools, with an obligation to appoint only Church of England communicants as masters, and to teach the Church catechism to all children. Certain objections were also made against the books being used in the schools, and that the catechism was not correctly taught. The complaints were largely founded, the Bishop admits in one letter, on the statements and authority of Mr. James, the first master at Middleton school. Mr. James had been appointed in 1819 at a salary of £100, and in June of that year, the Court was notified of his good conduct and efficiency in getting the schools well started. In 1820 he was permitted to start an evening school in the school buildings, after 5 p.m. In 1821, however, the agent had to report " very great dereliction of duty in neglecting the schools last winter during Mr. Stagg's absence ", and a severe reprimand was administered. In 1823, " having taken Orders ", he was allowed to leave at Christmas, but unfortunately and perversely he took with him all the books and documents relating to the schools and their foundation. In spite of many demands and requests, he obstinately refused to restore the papers, and Mr. Bainbridge was ordered by the Court to take severe steps to secure their return. Late in 1824, Mr. Bainbridge, acting on legal advice, was finally able to get back most of the papers in instalments, but a few were never recovered. This is the zealot who is quoted by the Bishop as his sole authority for the statement that the schools were built and endowed as Church of England schools. The Court reminded the Bishop that the schools were suggested by themselves, built at their sole expense, and salaries, etc., paid by the Company, but conceded that the early masters had been selected from Church of England members as an act of courtesy and convenience. The schools most certainly were not Church schools, although occasionally a part of the catechism had been taught in them. The Bishop eventually agreed that " all this does exactly show that these were *not* originally Church schools ", and after a list and samples of the books used had been sent to him, the Court notes its " gratification to find your Lordship has been pleased to state there is not a book upon that list which you would object to see in use in any of your own schools ". One can only feel that there was probably a sense of relief mixed with sarcasm in this minute, and a wish that the Bishop had listened less to gossip and taken more trouble to base his complaint on facts in the first case, and had not waited until 1849 to complain of an 1835 appointment. Later the Bishop again returned to his charges, but had to admit when pressed " that he made them from recollection, having left the relevant papers in the country ". The Court finally notified him " that they cannot consistently make any further material alteration in their schools, with

THE COMPANY'S DAY AND SUNDAY SCHOOLS 65

their duty towards the large body of men in their employ" and, after reminding him that the agreements made when they contributed £400 to the cost of the Weardale school, and subscriptions to the master's salary, had not been kept on his part, but that many miners' children had been compelled to attend catechism and sectarian teaching, etc., they closed the whole matter by handing over the Weardale schools entirely to him, and transferring their men on to Teesdale leases.

In 1858 the schools were reported as being in a highly satisfactory state, and it was proposed to "give the school children an occasional excursion treat". This was done, and there are notes that the outdoor treat was a great success, and alternatively that the present of 2s. to each child was very warmly received. In 1859 the Court notes with satisfaction " the high character given to all our schools by A. F. Forster, Esq., Assistant Commissioner for Education ". In appreciation of this report and the work the schoolmasters had done to merit it, the Court awarded a gratuity of £20 to each master. A plan for rebuilding the schools at Nent Head and Middleton at a cost of £2,000 each, was approved in November 1860, and a tablet in testimony to Robert Stagg, and his continual interest in the schools and exertions for their improvement, was ordered to be fixed in each. The inscription from Nent Head school has already been given.

The report of 1861 says the masters remain most zealous, and as the good reports of Government visitors continue to be received, the gratuity of £20 is repeated, and the next year is made a permanent addition to the salaries. The Company had not always been so fortunate in their masters. The example of James has already been given, who apparently after ordination worked and plotted to secure the schools to the Church. The first master at Nent Head had been dismissed after a short period as being an immoral character, and his successor was forty years old at his appointment, and is soon noted to be " not so good as we desire ". His reports were slightly improved, and to secure the man's interest in his job, the basis of payment was changed for a period from fixed salary to 3s. per child per quarter. This was apparently effective, and the master was soon restored to his old basis of payment. After twenty years' service he was sent to Middleton school for a month to study the efficient methods of a young master there, and after a further six years' service was retired with a gratuity of £50. Middleton had been far more fortunate in its masters. A master appointed in 1836 was only twenty-two years old but evidently a man of bright talents. After striking success in the school, he was promoted to schools inspector for the Company, and later made the schools examiner. His cousin was put under him to learn his methods, and was later appointed to Nent Head school. It was the invariable custom of the Company, not only in respect of their schoolmasters, but for clerks, smelters, agents, etc., to send them for short periods to other branches of the Company to study the methods of the best men they had, or even to undergo a period of active training to fit them better for their job. In this way the great smelt mills at Eggleston, near Middleton-in-Teesdale, became the " school " for their smelters, and Nent Head the training ground for miners and surveyors.

The curriculum of the schools is nowhere fully defined in the minutes, but from the many references it is clear that the main emphasis was put upon reading, writing, and a fair standard of arithmetic, with the Bible used not only as a reading book, but studied as literature also. For the girls there was more emphasis on religious teaching and also some time given to needlework and house crafts. After leaving the elementary school, the boys had the opportunity of attending evening classes and lectures of a more technical kind, and libraries were provided with a very wide selection of books both technical and literary which, according to frequent reports, were very well used—" thanks to the habits of diligent reading acquired in the schools ".

Libraries had been provided from the earliest days of the Company, in the Friends' Meeting Houses built in all the mining areas, but the books provided there were entirely confined to religious works, journals of Friends, etc. From the middle of the eighteenth century the Company's agents had been encouraged to loan books to the men who could read, and by 1800 chemical apparatus and books were provided to the agents for the better instruction of their assistants. This apparatus was taken into the evening classes, held sometimes in the Company's offices and sometimes in the schoolroom. In 1833 the Company, far in advance of all other mining concerns in the country, built

Plate V The Assay House and Stores at Nent Head Smelt Mill.

Plate VI Cornish stamps at Rampgill Mine dressing floor, Nent Head. Stamps were used at all the company's mills in Alston Moor by 1738.

Plate VII   The Garrigill road and the upper South Tyne Valley.

Plate VIII   Coins with "Roses and Plumes", made in the early eighteenth century from silver supplied by the London Lead Company: 5s, 2s 6d, 1s and 6d, all of them known locally as "Quaker shillins".

assay offices and laboratories at Middleton, Stanhope and Nent Head, where all ores could be analysed as they came from the mines, and all processes in the smelt mills and refineries checked and adjusted day by day. Neighbouring lead producers report on many occasions that the London Lead Company's lead and silver are of the best quality on the market, and that this is largely because they test all ores and keep separate the produce from different mines, adjusting furnaces and processes to each different type of ore. In order to ensure a supply of skilled assay chemists and metallurgists, and to keep up research on new methods, the Company invited Professor James Finley Weir Johnston, Reader in Chemistry and Mineralogy in Durham University, author of the very popular *Chemistry of Common Life*, to give a course of chemical lectures to all the agents and assistants at Middleton during the winter of 1834. £40 was spent on new and special apparatus and £21 on a collection of special minerals (later presented to the University), while Professor Johnston was paid £105 for his course. To continue the work thus begun, £30 was spent on books for the libraries at Nent Head and Middleton, with which the men could follow the lecture subjects further. Later, in 1845, the Court record that " the most promising and intelligent of the younger clerks are sent for instruction in Chemistry, etc., to Newcastle, at such times of the year as they can best be spared, also they are occasionally sent on journeys to inform themselves by visiting other establishments ". These clerks were at Newcastle the pupils of Dr. T. Richardson, who was Lecturer in Chemistry at the College of Medicine, and succeeded Professor Johnston in 1856 as Reader in Chemistry in the University. In the course of his training of the Company's men, he made some suggestions for improvements in their metallurgical processes, which the Company acknowledged with handsome gifts, on more than one occasion, of 100 guineas, but later he claimed that certain processes, particularly in ore calcining, that they were using were his own processes, and that the Company should pay a royalty for them. They were able to show that the calcining furnaces had been in use by them for over fifty years and at least forty years before his suggestions were made. However, in general recognition of the benefit their men had derived from his teaching, they gave him a piece of plate to cost £110. By this strict attention to the training of their technical staff, and constant expenditure on apparatus, and particularly to the extent of many thousands of pounds annually on large-scale experiments, the Company maintained for over two centuries its unique position for purity of its products and economy of production. As early as 1696 and as late as 1900 we hear, and at all times in between, that the market prefers the lead and silver of the London Lead Company to any other it can get.

Fig 3 Nent Head reading room, underground agent's house and new school (1863).

The encouragement of reading among the workmen has already been mentioned, in the early days being fostered by the agents loaning books to a few selected people. By 1800 the Company began to give fairly regular grants to the agents for purchase of books for loan to the men, and also to subscribe to several small libraries, started mostly in the Company's offices. In 1820, libraries were well established in all the centres, at first in the schools, then later in reading rooms built for the purpose. The subscriptions to Nent

Head and Middleton libraries were usually £15 or £20, and to smaller libraries at Dufton, Garrigill, etc., £5 or £10. In the next few years the following libraries were founded and subscribed to regularly—Garrigill, Stanhope, Dufton, Hilton, Lunehead, Egglestone, Harewood, Lune Forest, and Tyne Head. By 1850 the Company were subscribing annually to sixteen libraries in their area, and over a long period of years more than £100 per annum was being spent by them on new books alone.

A reading room was built at Nent Head in 1833, rebuilt in 1855 and enlarged in 1859, and a case of mineral specimens from the various mining fields added. Similar reading rooms were also built at Middleton and Stanhope. In donations to the reading rooms and libraries, over £600 was given by the Court.

Among many recreational activities encouraged by the Company, games, cricket clubs, garden societies, etc., the bands stand out as being typical of the northern Pennine area. Nearly all the older villages of the Dales areas of Yorkshire and Durham had, until recently, a little " Band Room " tucked away somewhere. The same applied to the Company's villages. The first bands officially recognized were at Nent Head about 1820 ; and the Company gave an annual donation of £5 towards it. In 1825, bands were started in Long Marton, Stanhope, Garrigill, and other villages, and in 1835 the Company subscribed £28 9s. 6d. towards new instruments for the Nent Head band. At that time there were bands on the Company's subscription list at Middleton, Nent Head, Garrigill, Lunehead, Romald Kirk, Dufton, Mickleton, Eggleston and Stanhope. Occasionally the £5 annual subscription was increased to £10 or £15 when new or extra instruments were wanted, and on two occasions " towards the dresses of the band ". The last entry specifically relating to a band is in 1862 when the Court presented a drum to Middleton band. The band, however, remained a prominent feature of the village life until well into the twentieth century. It always led the Sunday School children and workmen on any occasion of rejoicing, besides providing music at the cattle show, flower show, and innumerable other public occasions.

The Company's concern for education had, as they state on several occasions in the minutes, a very practical bearing on the regulation of the industry, by providing a steady supply of men of character and intelligence for positions in the offices and agencies, and as " overmen " in the mines. The mines organization had been systematized at a very early date, on a basis of regular inspection and oversight of all work by the general agent for each district, and by such members of the Court who had skill in mining and were appointed to make a tour of the centres. After the sale of the Welsh and Derbyshire mines in 1792 and the purchase of a large number of new leases in the North, this system of occasional visits from London proved inadequate, and a new organization had to be evolved. The head of affairs for the North was the general agent of the Company, residing at first at Nent Head and later at Middleton, who was in fact both general secretary and manager for the northern districts. Under him were appointed district agents, one at Nent Head and others at various smaller centres, Stanhope, Hilton, Dufton, Lunedale, etc. They acted as local managers, and were men of practical mining experience, appointed from among the higher ranks of the miners, and they were mainly responsible for the conduct of the mining operations. At the same time other agents were appointed, a little lower in the scale of responsibility, as mill agents, in charge of smelting, washing agents in charge of the ore dressing, and underground agents responsible to the district agent for the underground work of all kinds. All these were appointed by districts, either large or small, and were responsible through the district agent to the general agent and the Court. For the conduct of each particular mine, a new type of official was created in 1816 in the mine " overman ", a person selected from the miners themselves, for his skill and character. He was finally responsible for the work and safety of the mine, responsible as the go-between for men and Court, and looked to to encourage friendly relations and right dealings in the mine. The most concise view of the various duties can perhaps be had from a report about 1820, as follows :—

Much has been effected from time to time, as occasion offered for improving and rendering more perfect the distribution, division, and general economy of labour both in the mines, the mills, and in every other Department, but the most important improvement made in the management of the concern, was the

TRAINING OF OVERMEN, AND MINES COUNCIL

introduction of *Mine Overmen*, taken from the ranks. Prior thereto, the mine workings were visited by an Agent very rarely, leaving the miners to play tricks, and take advantage of all kinds ; but the daily and hourly inspection of overmen, puts a final close to all such, with an improved economy which scarcely admits of being fully estimated.

As the Overmen too, are always selected from the best and most skillful workmen, great encouragement is thereby held out for general good conduct, by the hope of preferment ; and what is of infinite moment, the less skillful miners are constantly put into more skillful and safer modes of performing their work, by the daily oversight and instruction they receive from their overlookers ; and not less is the benefit of having thus a body of men in full training for Mine Agencies ;—and also as an effectual check on all chance of partiallity being shown in fixing the Bargain Rates. For when the opinions are given for each bargain by all the Agents and overmen, partiallity is out of the question and it is equally out of the question for any essential error being perpetuated either in fixing those rates or in undertaking improper new operations in the face of so searching and so practical a mining Council. This Mining Council is formed each quarter by the union of the Agents from *each District*, and of the residential Overmen of the Mines to be inspected ; who together examine and *report separately* on every working in progress, or that is proposed as a fitting object for trial ; as well as on the economy of and proper use of the wood, and of every other material consumed in the Mines ;—also generally the state of the repairs and good and safe condition of the mines when so viewed.

As it is not in the power of the Superintendent (General Agent) to pass through the mines except on special occasions, the District Agents were established, and the whole of them do pass through *all* the Mines each quarter, and give the Superintendent their separate report in writing, of the state of the workings, and of the Bargain prices, which will give every possible security to the Company, stimulate each Agent to the utmost exertion, and carry into the whole concern, the advantage of all the mining abilities of their Mining Agents.

It is most remarkable from the above account of the organization, how the Company built up its management from the ranks, on a very sound democratic basis of skill and character. It was possible to rise from miner to overman, then to agent, district agent, and finally to superintendent. This was not merely a possibility, but was actual fact, as the appointments made after 1820 demonstrate. No outside person was brought into the work, *all* officials started with the Company as boys, and rose through successive positions to the highest. The result must have been a remarkable unity of feeling throughout a large organization, and a constant sympathetic understanding between miners and agents, all being of the same stock and all coming from the ranks. Such a democracy could only be based on a sound education and maintained by emphasis on character. Not the least pleasing aspect of the Mining Council must have been the impossibility of favouritism, and the assurance of absolute fairness and justice in the fixing of working places and the rates of pay. Behind this organizational scheme, of course, is the long experience that most of the Court and officials had of the methods of business in the Society of Friends, and to some extent the London Lead Company offers us a closer parallel in business to the Quaker way of organizing than any other concern of which we have knowledge.

No actual figures have been given yet to indicate the size of organization being discussed. Between 1815 and 1865 the number of miners at work underground (i.e. " pickmen ") varied between 600 and 1,000, with an average over that period of 865 for each year, and though there is no record of the number of boys, washery hands, carters, smelters, and estate servants, etc., these must have run into several hundreds more. The mines that the Company worked in this northern area are given in the following list, which is by no means complete, as it does not include veins worked by cross-cut from a neighbouring vein, or many of the smaller isolated mines and trials which were worked for periods of perhaps only ten or twenty years. These are the mines that were worked for the better part of a century at the least, and some of them for over 180 years :—

NENT HEAD DISTRICT.

Rampgill	Scaleburn
Guddamgill Moss	Middlecleugh
Longcleugh	Carrs South vein
Small Cleugh	Capelcleugh
Cowslitts	Cowhill
Hangingshaw	Carrs East vein
Blaegill	Nentsberry
Dowpot Syke	Dowgang

TRAINING OF OVERMEN, AND MINES COUNCIL

   Brownley Hill   Wellgill
   Brigghill Burn   Shawfoot
   Redgroves   Handsome Mea

GARRIGILL AND TYNEHEAD.
   Longhole Head   Browngill
   Thortergill   Bentyfield
   Cowperdyke Heads   Tynebottom
   Garrigill Burn   Old Groves
   Hundyshaw Bridge   Crossgill
   Crossgill Head   Taylors Grove
   Galligill Syke   Windybrae
   Tynehead   Clargill Head
   Tyne Green   Guttergill

WEARDALE.
   Whitfield Brow   Wager Burn
   Bollihope Burn   Middlehope
   Ireshope   Cornish Hush
   South Green
and a moiety of 30 small mines purchased 1790.

DERWENT AREA.
   Shildon   Ramshaw
   Hunstanworth   Feldon
   Muggleswick   Fellgrove
   Beldon Shields   Jeffries Rake
   Whiteheaps

TEESDALE AND LUNEHEAD.
   Ashgill Head   Bleagill
   Coldberry   Coldberry Skears
   Redgroves   High Dyke
   East Rake   Wiregill
   Little Eggleshope   Flakebrigg
   Lunehead   Manorgill
   Scraith Head   Flushie Mea
   High Dyke   Lodge Syke
   Hudshope Head   Dusty Gill
   Sharnberry   Birkdale

WESTMORLAND.
   Hilton Fell   Dufton Fell
   Silverband   Scoredale

  This is no mean list when the note on **agents** is born in mind, with the instruction that agents must make the inspection of *all* mines once each quarter. Over the same period, 1815 to 1865, the total amount of smelted lead sold from the northern mines of the Company was 203,000 tons, and 2,405,000 ounces of silver were refined from it. Of the immense advances made by the Company in technical processes during the production of all this lead and silver, this is no place to speak in detail, but it can be said at once that they were the largest single contributors to the science and technique of mining and smelting of lead and refining of silver in Europe during that period. It may also be fair to add that their experiments in social and business organization are worth an equally high position in the history of industrial development.

NOTES TO CHAPTER III

A report on the Greenwich Hospital Estates in Alston Moor was made to the Admiralty, July 1821 by the Secretary, Edward Hawke Locker. Many of his recommendations were based upon the practice of the London Lead Company, their lessees. e.g. "But there is still much want of a parochial library ... it should contain books of scientific information to which the miners may have access." He also made many suggestions for improving transport between the Moor and Newcastle.

Raistrick, A. "The London (Quaker) Lead Company Mines in Yorkshire." *Northern Mines Research Society, Memoirs*, 1972, for an account of the mines in Yorkshire.

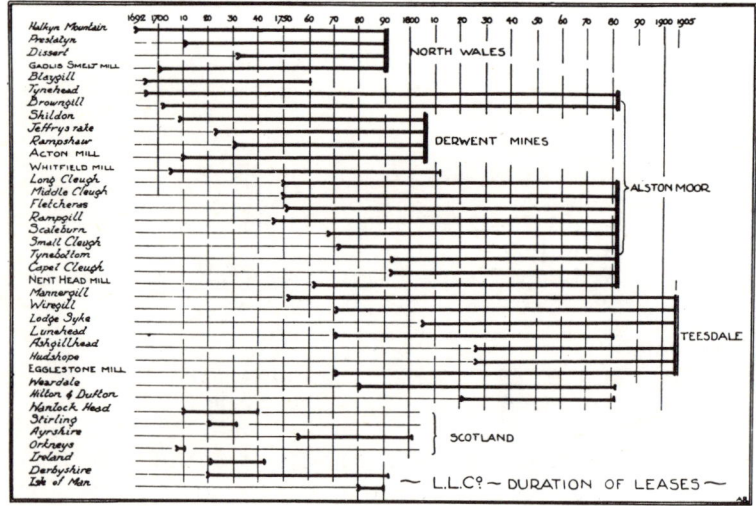

Fig 4 Diagram showing the duration of the London Lead Company's leases.

CHAPTER IV

Transport during the early period—Pack-horse Roads and Transport—Road and Canal Works in Derbyshire—Road and Canal Works in Alston Moor—Railways, Alston Moor and Teesdale.

DURING the earlier period of the Company, when still working as the Ryton Company and the Mines Royal Copper of Wales between 1692 and 1705, the isolation was less acute than when the estates in the North were being consolidated, as the main centres of operation were at Gadlis and Ryton. Both sites were within reach of tidal waters, and little difficulty was experienced in keeping up close shipping connection with London, other than the risks then incident to all shipping. It was easy in time of high food prices to return cargoes of food bought in the London market to the Welsh and northern centres, by the boats that were carrying back bone ashes, tools, and other stores for the Company's works. The books of the Court contain many reports from district managers that the price of meal or bread is high, and the decision that a boat load of rye or corn be sent down, to be sold at cost price to the miners and their families. One reason for this policy was perhaps not so altruistic as at first sight may appear, although it was both far-seeing and sound; the Company endeavoured as far as possible to maintain a constant rate of wages, and at the same time to offset rises in the cost of living by providing cheaper food from London, so that the actual exchange value of the wages was not lessened when local food prices rose. This policy was very difficult and the mechanism somewhat cumbersome and, late in the eighteenth century, wages were more directly related to the cost of food, though in times of food shortage the Company still sent supplies to all its districts from London.

At Gadlis, the early Company built its new smelt mill in 1702, complete with several houses for the officials and higher employees, and regulated hours of work and the conduct of its workpeople within fairly strict limits. The Court minutes note that the head furnace man is to be engaged for three years at £40 a year, with a house and four loads of coals provided; the blacksmith and his son are engaged at 10s. per week, again with house and coals, and several others of the workpeople are provided, some with house and some with coals. The agent is given both house, coals, and a horse, with generous allowance for his journeys to London and to other districts. Letters of instruction and business correspondence of many kinds have an old-world charm and courtesy about them that give a strong hint of Friendly care and concern for their employees. A letter to a new clerk working at Gadlis finishes :—

> This is what occurs at present to inform you of, so leaving you to the Protection of the Almighty, we wish you a good journey and prosperity to attend your affairs, we rest
> your Loving friends,
> . . . .

A report on general conditions at Gadlis in 1708 says that the workmen are in good order, not allowed to swear, visit alehouses, or bring drink to the works, except from their own families. They are called to work by beat of drum at 6 a.m., and discharged at 12 noon, recalled at 1 p.m., and discharged for the night at 6 p.m. The report continues with the result of enquiries that show that the Company is in good repute, and the miners and workpeople are in very friendly relations with all around and are well liked and respected. Pennant, the historian of that part of North Wales, writing in the late eighteenth century, says that the Quaker Company " flourished with a most fair reputation ". As the mines serving Gadlis were in the adjacent Halkyn mountain district, the problem of road transport was never very acute, and most of the Company's activity was devoted to improvements of smelting methods, and to regulation of their workpeople.

In the North, the cupola at Ryton was within three miles of Newcastle, and as most of the ore used was purchased at first from independent miners, there was little need for rapid development of other than purely business relations. The agent at Ryton, Charles Alsopp, was an active Friend, often representing his Monthly and Quarterly Meeting at Yearly Meeting, and regularly entertaining visiting Friends and ministers at his home. He visited the neighbouring works of Ambrose Crowley at Winlaton, and no doubt was actively impressed and inspired by the workmen's court and other "advanced" aspects of the Crowley works. Although Crowley was not a Friend, he was of Friends family and would have much in common with Alsopp and Wright, who visited him on several occasions. In his dealings with the miners of Alston Moor, Alsopp was brought up against the problems of isolation. The earliest mines the Company possessed in the area were around Tynehead, a place still very remote from all traffic, and inaccessible for a great part of the winter. Ore was carried from Tynehead by pack horse train to Ryton, over thirty-five miles of wild mountains and moors. Alsopp soon moved to improve the way, and spent some amount of time and money in developing a good road. Food was carried back by the pack train from Newcastle market to Tynehead, along with tools, clothing, etc.

The " pack horses " remained in use until the main road system was nearly completed, about 1826, and even then were continued between some of the out-of-the-way mines and smaller villages. The horses or ponies used were known locally as the " carrier galloways ", or, for shortness, as the " galls ". A pack train was made up of twelve to thirty animals, which moved along in single file, with one " gall " always the leader. The leader had a set of bells on his harness, the custom being one large bell in the middle of the collar and three small spherical bells on each side, the tradition being that these gave warning of the approach of a pack train in the narrow roads where passing was difficult. The custom is still remembered in most parts of the Pennines in the way in which children in their games will yoke up a long string of boys in tandem, to run as " belled horses ". There used to be very keen competition among the boys to have the post of " bell horse " or leader. The train of ponies generally had two attendants, a man and a boy, or more if the journey was to take a day or two and packs would have to be taken off at night and replaced next morning. The strings of " galls " usually travelled by fairly straight, well-known routes across the hills, the softer places being set with large stones, still a well-known feature of our Pennine " pack horse roads ". Where the track rises up a steep brow, being unpaved, a deep gully is soon worn which, in winter, becomes the bed of a stream. As one track became undesirable in that way, the " galls " would pass to one side and begin to make a parallel track. On the hill slopes above most of the mines and smelt mills these parallel sunk ways are still visible. It is obvious that the travelling by pack train was entirely dependent on the weather for speed, and that in bad winters the time taken, and consequently the food needed by the " galls " on a journey, were both increased. With softer ground, the loads had to be lighter, and so more ponies were used for the same bulk of goods carried. This explains why all carriage charges during the eighteenth century state the season of the year, as transport was nearly twice as costly in winter as in summer. Each " gall " carried from 2 to 3 cwt. The load was slung evenly on the animal's two sides, special saddles being used for the carriage of bulky goods like timber for the mines, or corn for the markets.

The policy of placing the smelt mills as near the mines and sources of fuel as possible, was adopted in order to reduce as much as possible the length of journey for the ore before it had been reduced in bulk and weight by smelting, but at the same time not to increase too much the journey of the coal for fuel. In the case of the removal from Ryton Mill to the Cupola Mill at Whitfield, the difference in transport costs is set out in the minutes, viz. :—

Alston Moor " all on horseback, the ways being inaccessible for a coach . . . " and on the way we saw Whitfield Mill, a place much used for smelting lead in hearths by help of water (power). Thos. Pattinson suggests it might be convenient for smelting slags. Rent about £7 or £8 per annum.

Five bings* of ore may yield about 1 fodder of lead and may be carried to Whitfield (from Alston Moor) for   0 13 4
the fodder of lead carried to Blaydon or Ryton........   0 13 4

                                                                                       1 6 8

* A bing is the common measure of ore for all purposes, and is about 8 cwt., while the " fodder " is a rather variable measure. In an early minute book of the Company, a table is inserted for the use of the clerks, which gives the following values of the fodder.

Newcastle fodder	2,352 lb.
London ,,	2,184 ,,
Stockton ,,	2,464 ,,
York ,,	2,505½ ,,
Hull ,,	2,340 ,,
Bawtry ,,	2,408 ,,
Wales ,,	2,400 ,,

Five bings ore carried to Ryton.....................	1	15	0
so there will be saved in carrying it to Whitfield......	0	8	4
The coals may be dearer at Whitfield than at Ryton for smelting so much ore..............................	0	1	4
so that a fodder of lead would be worked cheaper at Whitfield than at Ryton by........................	0	7	0

In 1706, as noted in another chapter, the Ryton Smelt Mill was surrendered on a long lease to the Blacketts, and Whitfield Smelt Mill purchased (and remained in work until 1816), followed in 1708 by the building of Acton Mill in the Derwent valley. In the case of Acton, the mill and mines were in the parish of Blanchland, a strong Church centre, and the Company, though working there for a century, were not able to enter very deeply into the life of the people outside the actual mine work. These mines were sold by the Company in 1806. Whitfield Mill, however, was in a different position altogether. Situated in West Allendale, it was fairly remote from Newcastle (thirty miles) in a sparsely populated area of very wide extent, but an area that had been visited by early Friends, and in which there was a Meeting settled. In 1703 Alsopp had married Lydia Brown at West Allendale Meeting, and in 1716 built Broadwood Hall, Allendale, as their home. Not far from Whitfield was the other Friends' settlement at Coanwood, and from the beginning of the Whitfield Smelt Mill, Coanwood was linked with it by leases of coal mines and peat cuttings, for fuel supply. In this way, two bodies of employees of the Company at the smelt mills and at the collieries, were brought together in places already well established as Friends' centres. It was possible in such circumstances for very close and Friendly connection to develop between employers and employees, and for a concern for the welfare of the workpeople to ripen quickly. With the establishment of Whitfield Mill, the Tynehead miners were able to bring their ore by easier roads to Whitfield, and to develop closer contact with their fellow employees. This led to increased interest in the Alston Moor area, and eventually was a strong factor in deciding the Company's interests in the North.

In 1709, with the Company taking up interests in the various mines in Scotland, the instructions to their visiting representatives make some points of their policy clear. In the case of the Orkneys, the agent is instructed to " take

Wm. Gibson from London and some miners from Newcastle to examine mines in the Islands of Mainland and How, and also island of Stronsa where Earl of Morton has a mine of silver . . .". They are also to enquire " likewise, what commodities these islands produce that may be vended here, likewise what commodities may be acceptable there. Also get what knowledge you can of seasons of fishing and sorts of Fish in Orkney and Shetland ".

Rather similar instructions on several journeys emphasize the habit of the Company to develop a local industry, fishing, agriculture, or stock rearing, when possible, alongside the mining in order to stabilize the living of their miners. This policy was very fully developed in the later periods at Nent Head and Middleton, where miners were encouraged to develop small-scale farming.

In the case of Wanlock Head, in South Scotland, the Company had interesting relations with an outside body of miners. In 1710 their leases of the Wanlock mines began to operate, smelt mills, refinery, houses, etc., being built on the spot, and a road transport developed with Edinburgh and Leith for the carriage of their lead and silver for sale or shipping. The Company showed its mining foresight in Wanlock, by planning long and deep drainage levels that would improve the prospects of the whole area, and by starting work on them almost at once. The independent miners of the rest of the leases on the area were benefited by these drainage levels, and were invited to come into loose association with the Company. The miners formed themselves into an association, the " Friendly Mining Society ", to prosecute the rest of the leases outside the London Lead Company's takes, and in 1721 the London Lead Company proposed direct amalgamation with them. The whole area was for several years worked jointly by the London Lead Company and the Friendly Mining Society. In 1727 the amalgamation was ended by friendly arrangement, and in 1731 the London Lead Company surrendered all their leases, passing over their mill and equipment to the Friendly Mining Society, which flourished for several years longer.

In Derbyshire, the policy of the Company is seen after 1721, in the very friendly relations they maintained not only with their own workpeople, but with small independent miners, purchasing their ore at fair prices, making advances of money and tools to needy miners, and occasionally giving considerable technical advice and help. The difficulties of transport had forced on the Company the policy of building a smelt mill in every locality as near as possible to the mines, in order that the less bulk and weight of smelted lead should have the longer and more tedious journey from the mill to the market. The Derbyshire mines near Matlock were situated at a considerable distance from the port of shipment, Hull, and consequently the Derbyshire area felt most acutely the problem of transport. The lead was for many years carried by pack horse train across the hills to Bawtry on the Idle, a tributary of the Trent, and carried from there to Hull in barges. At an early date, the Company's agent, Joseph Whitfield, made considerable grants towards the costs of improving roads along that line, and also spent some money on building new roads between the mines and their smelt mill at Ashover.

The earliest contributions to roads in the Derbyshire area were simple contributions of £50 or £100 towards the cost of new roads, or subscriptions to parishes towards the repairs needed to roads already existing. Between their own mines and smelt mills, the Company made new roads, mainly for pony transport, coal and wood being carried to the smelt mills and mines, and ore and lead carried the other way. There are many interesting reports and minutes relating to the pack train transport, largely arising out of difficulties of payment. In the early days, carriers were paid by the sack or pack, and in many cases are accused, and often rightly, of using small sacks and shallow baskets, so that the cost of carriage was often out of all proportion to the weight of goods handled. The remedy for this was the provision of standard measures at the smelt mills, into which coal and charcoal was delivered, a payment note being made out by the "checkweighman". In all accounts the carriage rates vary with the season, with further offsets for particularly bad weather. This is mainly due to the condition of the unmetalled tracks, which in winter were either stream courses or deep sloughs of mud, and sometimes even unpassable for ponies. To reduce winter carriage as much as was desirable to balance these conditions, it would have been necessary to maintain large stocks of ore, coals, charcoal, and timber, with considerably enlarged storage space, and it was not in most cases easy to provide this; hence the agents' immediate interest in the new metalled roads that to some extent were being made by the turnpike trusts. At a later period in Derbyshire, Joseph Whitfield, the Company's agent, appears as one of the promoters of a group of turnpike acts designed to link the mining areas with Chesterfield, then the great outward town for Derbyshire traffic. In 1766, Whitfield and others of the Company officials in Derbyshire appear as promoters, with many others, of a turnpike road from Ashover (the site of the Company's smelt mill) to join the Chesterfield to Mansfield turnpike. The preamble to the Act says the existing road is ruinous, and in several places very narrow, and cannot be properly amended, widened, or repaired . . . etc. The Court encouraged Whitfield to press on with the promotion of this Bill and subscribed liberally towards it. At the same time they were considering the possibility of a canal from Chesterfield to Stockwith on the Trent, and among the Company's papers is an estimate by Brindley of the probable cost of such a canal, and the saving in transport charges when it was completed. After a good deal of correspondence and a detailed survey, much of the cost of which was borne by the Company, an Act of Parliament was promoted " For making a Navigable Cut or Canal from Chesterfield, in the County of Derby, through or near Worksop and Retford, to join the River Trent, at or near Stockwith in the County of Nottingham." This Act was obtained in 1771, and the lead from Ashover was sent by that route and by the new turnpike during the later years of the Company's work in Derbyshire.

The papers dealing with the canal project are of many-sided interest, but among the many types of material they cover, perhaps the most germaine at the moment is the light they throw on the amount and cost of transport in this area. The first document is a letter to Joseph Whitfield from James Grimthorpe, relating to the amount of goods traffic up the Idle to Bawtry, the proposed terminus of the subsidiary canal.

Mr. Whitfield,   Bawtry July 30th 1769
Sir,
    Agreeable to your requests have sent you an account of the number of Tunns of Goods as near as I can calculate which have been sent down and brought up the River in the compass of one

year; the reason I did not take the last year is occasioned by my having some other Accounts relating to the Wharf which was not drawn out for want of which would have occasioned me more trouble than the preceeding one, and all the Years prior to that of 1767 contained more Tunns as the business at the Wharf has been gradually decreasing for a number of Years.

Lead and other Goods sent from and brought to Bawtry from January 1767 to January 1768.

	Tunns
6,420 pigs of Lead is 802 fodd. at 24 hundred is	962
684 barrells Red lead at 8 hundd. per barrell	273
Sundry other goods sent down	340
Sundry Goods brought up	1,730
Timber	57
Stone and Freestone	97
Mr Paul Smith has paid dues for	707
Mr Bingley do in his own boats	249
	4,415

Brindley was secured to give an estimate for the canal, and his scheme was based on the returns the traffic dues and savings would give on the capital cost. These figures he submitted to Whitfield, as follows :—

Mr. Brinleys Estimate for compleating the Canal from Chesterfield to Stockwith is near £100,000 N.B. He has from past experience in Works of the like kind formed his Calculations for Executing this nearly one Fourth higher than he has done before.

Calculation of Tonnage returns.

30,000	Tons of Coal for the Inland Country brought 24 miles on an average at 1½d p Ton p mile.		4,500
50,000	Tons of ditto to the Trent for supplying Lincoln Gainsboro Newark and the adjacent country at 3/- per Ton		7,500
	The River Donn proprietors sell their Coal at Gainsboro for 10s p Ton		
	It cost delivering into their boats	4 8	
	It cost Fright	4 3	
	Expence p Ton at Gainsboro	8 11	
	They take no Tonnage		
	Delivered into the Canal boats at	3 3	
	Tonnage	3 0	
	Fright say 36 miles at ½ p ton	1 6	
		7 9	
	Ours lower than theirs p ton	1 2	

LONDON LEAD COMPANY

3,000	Fudders of Lead from Chesterfield is 44 miles at 5/6	825
12,000	Tons of Lime to manure 3,000 Acres of Land at 4 Tons upon an acre carried 15 miles at 1d p Ton mile	750
2,000	Tons of do for buildings and land in Lincolnshire carried on an average 25 miles at 1d p Ton p mile	1,250
5,000	Tons of Roche Abbey stone and Steetley Stone, equal or superior in Quality to Portland stone and supposed to be the best in England for Millstones; Plaister, Marble, Clay, Bricks, Tiles, Earthenware, Rotten Stone, Callamy, Copperas, carried 18 miles at 1d p ton p mile	375
8,000	Tons of Malt, Corn, and alsorts of Grain, Cheese, Hemp, Flax, Iron, Oak, Fir, Timber, Deals, Liquors etc, carried 24 miles on an average at $1\frac{1}{2}$ p Ton mile	1,200
	Total return from carriage	£16,400

The Cut is proposed to be $28\frac{1}{2}$ feet wide within the Banks and each Bank 12 feet.

The Boats to be 70 feet long and 7 feet wide, to draw 3 feet water, 24 Tons Burthen.

Will take 6 men and 3 horses every 24 hours to Navigate each Boat, and its supposed each Boat will make a Voige in 4 days. It is supposed to measure from Bawtry to the Trent near Gainsboro 12 Miles and will cost £15,000.

This latter is a reference to a further scheme to improve and canalize the R. Idle from Bawtry to Gainsborough in continuation of the canal scheme.

During the discussions of the possible canal for Derbyshire, the opinion of a second engineer, Mr. Grundy, was secured, who proposed a more direct line for the canal. Brindley's scheme, however, was not only an easier route, with little tunnelling and less lock rises, but it passed through and served a larger number of towns and villages on the way, and so was likely to collect more traffic. On completion of the canal Brindley was proved to be right by the amount of relatively short distance local traffic that was carried. This canal passed through Staveley, Worksop and Retford as its principal towns, and through a great number of villages along its route, that were important in the growing iron industry.

ROAD AND CANAL WORKS IN ALSTON MOOR

Brindley was throughout his professional career brought in close contact with Friends in business. His earliest work as a millwright was concerned with the machinery of paper and silk mills, but in 1756 he became a friend of the Wedgwood family of potters, and erected for them their first flint crushing mills. His friendship with Josiah Wedgwood was continued throughout his life and was cemented by his appointment as the engineer of the Grand Junction canal, connecting the Mersey, Trent and Severn, of which Wedgwood was the chief promoter. In his work on steam engines, Brindley spent some time at Coalbrookdale with the Darbys, the Quaker ironmasters, who made the iron parts of his various steam engines. The Darbys supplied the steam engine used by the London Lead Company at the Mill Close Mine, Derbyshire, and Abraham Darby and Joseph Whitfield were close friends, meeting not only on mining and engineering business but on the business of Friends. It was probably this connection that introduced Brindley to the Company as engineer for the proposed canal. Later, Brindley was invited to make the survey and became the engineer of the Leeds and Liverpool canal, promoted in 1768 by John Hustler and other members of the Bradford Meeting of the Society of Friends. Brindley's assistant on that work was a Friend, who finally carried out the greater part of the scheme, as Brindley became more and more busy in various parts of the country. As in the railway development, Friends played their part in the promotion of canals, during the period when Brindley was the premier canal engineer.

During the maximum period of the Company's activity in Alston Moor, they turned again to the idea of the cheapness of water transport, and joined in the promotion of surveys and schemes for a canal from Newcastle through the Tyne valley to Carlisle, which would have been joined by their merchandise somewhere near Haydon Bridge near the mouth of the Allendales. This scheme was never put in practice, although detailed plans and specifications were prepared. Partly in anticipation of it, the Company joined the Blackett-Beaumont proprietors of Allendale in laying out and completing a road up East Allendale, with a branch into Nent Head and one into Weardale, for the easy carriage of their lead to the canal.

With the consolidation of properties in the North, following the 1790 sales of Derbyshire and Welsh leases, the Company embarked on a period of active road building, to link up their estates in Alston Moor, Weardale, Teesdale, Swaledale and Westmorland. Reference has already been made to the isolation and the difficult nature of this country, and it was essential, if the agents were to visit all the centres regularly, that roads which would be fairly usable in winter should be made. The cost of carriage of ore from the mines to the smelt mills, and lead from the mills to the shipping wharf on the Tyne at Stella, was almost prohibitive in bad weather, and impossible for a great part of the winter, so long as the pack horses had to make their way across the moors by ill-defined and unsurfaced tracks. Between 1790 and 1810, the Company on several occasions defined its policy of building a network of serviceable roads, and under the stimulus of Robert Stagg, appointed mining agent for the North in 1778, and his son Joseph Stagg who succeeded him in 1808, this policy was translated into fact. Stagg made many reports to the Court of Assistants, in which, he invariably said " though the Company must never expect to see any direct return on the capital they advanced towards making and repairing roads and bridges, yet they would derive an ample return for the outlay—in the reduction in the rates of carriage of lead, stores, etc.—in keeping down the rate of wages by facilitating the ample supply of provisions and necessities for the workpeople—and by economizing the time of the agents, etc., in their journeys from mine to mine, and district to district ".

The first task undertaken by the Company was to report upon, and later indict, all roads used by the Company that were not properly repaired by the turnpike authorities, after proper representation had been made. By actively pursuing this policy, the turnpike roads, particularly the west road from Newcastle through Hexham and the road up Weardale, were soon considerably improved. In most cases where improvements were forced, the Company made generous grants towards the cost, e.g. :—

1813 £200 towards road from Stanhope to Newcastle via Dipton.
£10 towards Bridge at Cowes Hill, Weardale.

ROAD AND CANAL WORKS IN ALSTON MOOR

1815 £100 towards road from Stanhope to Egglestone. township of Frosterly determined to 1 against the indictment of this road, wherein failed.)
This road was afterwards in large part rebuilt by the Co.

1816 £20 road Middlehope to Westgate (Weardale).
£50 further for road Stanhope to Egglestone.

In this way, by similar grants, they contributed to the improvement of practically every road and main bridge in the district. (See Map 3.) A series of smaller cross roads between their various mines and mills were planned about this time, and gradually carried out, partly by their own labour, when their cost comes within the ordinary estate accounts and is difficult to trace in full detail, and partly by " relief " labour, an interesting anticipation of very recent state action.

1816 £50 to Distress Committee in Alston—to be spent in labour on such parts of Roads as may be pointed out, and £50 now promised if distress continue—on same conditions.

In 1817 a new line of road up Teesdale was proposed which, if effected, would enable the Company to carry ore throughout the winter months. One has to remember here that many of the mines were well above 2,000 feet above sea level, on the heights of the Pennines, and that apart from being snowed up for weeks on end, the old trackways frequently served as the main watercourse in time of excessive rain and melting of the snows. The new road was designed and later carried out in such a way as to avoid the most serious drifting of the snow, and to follow a line of easy drainage, well above the stream floods. The road over the fells to Dufton was made " and is so easy of access, that a saving of 1/6 per bing (8 cwt.) in Ore carriage has taken place—this will repay the cost in 18 months ". A bigger main road was built from Brough-under-Stainmoor, across Lunehead to Middleton, saving fourteen miles in the journey Dufton to Middleton, the old journey being Dufton to Garrigill and Garrigill to Middleton, or via Brough to Barnard Castle ; the new road being direct.

By 1823 over £1,500 had been given in grants to repairs of smaller roads, and an almost equivalent sum spent in making new cross roads. Along with the Greenwich Hospital Commissioners, the Company decided to take the advice of Macadam on a comprehensive " Grand Line of Roads " through Weardale, Teesdale, and Alston Moor, granting £5,000 towards the first cost and later making further grants of £500 for the extra cost of part of the road over Yad Moss, and a further £500 to supplement an " inadequate grant of £1,200 ". With the completion of this scheme, the agent reports to the Court that " the superintendent can now make the tour of all the Districts either on horseback or in carriage, in two days ". A saving in the number of work-horses is also reported, and a saving of one day in every four weeks to the three agents. Although, as Stagg so frequently insisted, the capital expended in roads was not directly returned, yet time after time the agents report to the Court that the gains in easier regulation, oversight and visiting of the mines, and in cheaper and more reliable transport, are of very great value in the affairs of the Company, and there can be no doubt that the policy was wise and proved entirely successful. In the fifty years between 1815 and 1865, the Company spent £12,500 in direct grants to road schemes, and about an equivalent amount in their own direct labour on the cross roads. The whole district is to-day still reaping advantage from their foresighted policy, though many of the major roads are now passing into county and national administration.

The effect of the new roads on the cost of carriage of ore and materials from and to their own mines, is clearly stated in many minutes of the Court and in the agents' reports. The whole department was considerably reorganized when the road scheme was adopted, and teams of carriers were substituted for casual labour. A note in 1813 says:—

In the carriage department an immense saving has been effected by Mr. Stagg, principally by inducing a new set of carriers to enter the service ; and classing the whole into 1st, 2nd, and 3rd rate men, according to their conduct and exertions— prior to the new arrangement the carriers were in the constant habit of standing out for higher rates—or " sticking " (the local term for rebellion). This was annihilated, and for instance, he found on entering office, the carriage of Lead from Stanhope Mill, costing 1/10d. per piece (i.e. 1½ cwt.)—and the Ore carriage from Middlehope at 4/6d. per bing (8 cwt.), and the carriers sticking for higher rates. These were speedily lowered to 11d. per piece, and the ore to 2/6d. per bing—and a similar reduction was accomplished in these and all other carriages at the several Mills, etc. These changes could not be effected without incurring great personal abuse, and no little odium, among the carriers.

The regular reports show the savings made by better organization, as follows :—

Aug. 1815   The saving in the carriage of Lead, ore, etc., is estimated at £1,543 this year.
March 1816 The saving in carriage of the lead this year is estimated at a further £1,451.
1819   A further saving of £300 per year has been made in carriage by sending ore to Eggleston instead of to Stanhope Mill for smelting.
1826   Carriage rates are to be advanced in the winter months if considered necessary.
1835   The saving in carriage by the employment of the Railway (Wear Valley line) is £700 to £800 per year.
1836   The policy of increasing the rates paid to carriers to keep them on the roads in competition with the railways, is justified at present.
1844   Note of impositions of the Railway Company in the rates for carriage of silver.
Agreement with Waggon Company to take all our silver by road.
New agreement with the Railway Company for carriage of our Lead, just received.
" Lead can now be sent with equal facility and about the same cost, from Teesdale to Newcastle or from Stanhope to Stockton."

Along with the reorganization of the overground haulage, the " drawing " of ore underground was reconsidered. It had for a long time been the custom of the Company to let contracts to individual horse keepers, for the contract of bringing or " drawing " the cut ore from the mine face out to the bank. This necessitated a separate contract for each mine, and was a constant source of trouble through complaints by the miners against the drawers, and the drawers against the miners. In 1815 the Company decided for a year to draw the ore from all Teesdale mines with their own horses and men, and at the end of the year the office reported a net saving of £521 on the drawing contracts. In 1816, direct Company labour was put to the drawing in Alston Moor leases, and there a saving of £350 was made. From that time the Company did all the drawing, and quickly became aware of difficulties in the layout and arrangement of the mines that they had not previously experienced. The surveyors were put to the job of resurveying and regrading levels, etc., and on the completion of the business, iron rail lines were introduced into all the longer drawing levels. In 1821, after four years' trial, the accountants reported that the use of iron rails saved, on the average, £250 in the drawing costs. The results in the Company's mines were so striking that iron waggon ways underground were soon after in use throughout the northern mining fields.

As might be expected, during the nineteenth century when steam railways were being built in most parts of the country, serious consideration was given to the possibility of desirable lines and services through the Company's mining areas. In 1817 the iron rails introduced to the drawing levels were extended as light waggon ways to all the Company's washing floors and to the smelt mill yards, and the success of them and the saving effected by them predisposed the Company to favour similar railways, but also weighted their experience in favour of horse-drawn trains. In November 1819, a railway was proposed by Edward Pease and other Friends, to run from Stockton, through Aukland, to Evenwood Bridge. This was one of the principal coal mining areas belonging to the Bishop of Durham, and at Evenwood the Duke of Cleveland had his lead smelting mill, the Gaunless mill, which was already connected by good roads with the Company's mills and mines in Teesdale. The Company were asked to subscribe to this railway, and to carry their lead from Eggleston to railhead at Evenwood, and thus by rail to Stockton. After due consideration the Court declined to subscribe to the scheme, but stated no reason, though one suspects that already they had in mind the Tees Valley railway. This (the Evenwood-Stockton) was the first line proposed by Edward Pease and the Darlington Friends, and was roughly along a line previously selected by Brindley for a canal and by Rennie in 1812 for a waggon way. The Parliamentary Bill was promoted in 1819 and again in 1820, but was defeated each time, and only passed in a modified form as the Stockton-Darlington Act, in 1821.

In 1828 the Newcastle to Carlisle Railway was proposed, the Act being obtained in 1829, and the Court minuted the reports of their agents as to the estimated advantages of the line for the conveyance of their lead, which would have to be carried by road from Alston Moor to the Tyne valley near Haydon Bridge. This railway again followed the line of a canal proposed in 1817 but never carried out. The ore from Weardale was sent by the Stanhope and Shields railway in 1835, but there were long negotiations and disputes before suitable carriage rates were agreed upon.

In 1845 a line was proposed to pass up Weardale from Stanhope, by Wearhead and Nent Head, to Alston, but after discussion of advantages and difficulties the scheme was dropped, and a branch line built from Haltwhistle on the Newcastle to Carlisle line, up the valley of the South Tyne, to Alston. This line was opened for traffic in 1852 and the Company's ore was sent from Nent Head by road to Alston, and there entrained.

The Court gave their support to a railway from Darlington into the Tees valley via Eggleston, and this railway was completed in 1867. Throughout the whole period of railway discussions the Company emphasized time after time their entire satisfaction with the efficiency of their road systems. Their roads were maintained in good enough condition and surface to allow the use of carts between all their mining centres and the railheads, and even to allow cartage of timber and materials to their remotest mines.

NOTES TO CHAPTER IV

Monkhouse, F. J. " The Transport of Lead and Silver from Langley Castle to Newcastle, 1768 to 1779." *Proc. Soc. Antiquaries, Newcastle upon Tyne.* 4th series, IX, No. 6, 1940, 176-186. A problem which also affected the London Lead Company.

CHAPTER V

The Social Policy of the Company—The Charter of the Governor and Company—Ryton Company and Mines Royal of Wales—The " Quaker Lead Company "—The " Quaker " Coinage—The Welsh Concerns, 1730-90—The Company in Derbyshire, 1721-90—Scotland, 1709-30—The Later Years of the Company, 1882-1905.

THE preceding chapters give a picture of the London Lead Company as a large employer with a concern for the well-being of his workpeople. A close examination of the history of the Company throughout the two centuries of its existence suggests that the social policy was the product mainly of three factors :—

(*a*) The natural isolation of most of its areas of activity was dependent on the distribution of the lead ore deposits. In this country they are confined mainly to two groups of rocks, the carboniferous limestone which forms the " backbone " of the Pennines and parts of the Halkyn mountains, North Wales, and the silurian rocks of the southern uplands of Scotland, with the older ordovician rocks of Central and North Wales. At the time of formation of the Company, and for more than a century later, these areas were almost untraversed by roads and were most difficult of access from any of the larger areas of population. Any large body of miners had thus to be provided against the worst effects of isolation, remoteness from markets, and dearness of food. This remoteness was only lessened during the nineteenth century with the general spread of turnpike roads across country, and finally by the development of railways.

(*b*) Early experience of the value of healthy and contented workpeople and a realization of the dangers of discontent leading to "rebellion", chartism, etc., when wages were forced to a low level, and became inadequate to maintain even the simplest standard of living. By meeting as far as possible the principal " needs ", both physical and mental, of their workpeople in any area, violent wage fluctuations and labour difficulties were avoided, and a constant willingness to discuss conditions and make adjustments prevented strikes.

THE SOCIAL POLICY OF THE COMPANY

(c) The strong Quaker element present in the Court and among the officials of the Company, ensured an increased sensitivity to the condition and needs of the workpeople, so that reports of their condition and suggestions for their improvement were always sure to receive both earnest and favourable discussion in the Court.

The enlightened policy that was encouraged by these factors was made possible of achievement by the financial success of the concern as a business—the Court could afford to spend money on roads, health, housing, education, etc., because its business was sound. Actually the very services established in this way became a source at least of saving to the Company, and proved in the end to be a very sound financial investment. In the case of the roads, built at great expense during a time of difficulty and depression, the saving on carriage alone, when mining improved, soon amounted to over a thousand pounds a year. The health services saved the Company a great loss of time and labour during the cholera and influenza epidemics, when neighbouring concerns were seriously handicapped. This saving of expense through wise spending is the keynote to all the Company's technical progress. Edward Wright had spent many years and much money on perfecting a new process of lead smelting and refining before 1700, and for the next two hundred years the Company never ceased to grant large sums of money for experimental work on all its processes. Time after time it is reported that a new method of work has been adopted, with a resultant saving of expenditure or increased productivity that in a few years repaid all the costs.

This willingness to experiment and insistence on technical progress is characteristic of many of the early Quaker industrialists, and no doubt was a main factor in leading to the expansion and success of their enterprises, which made their extended social work possible. In illustration one need only quote Abraham Darby, ironmaster of Coalbrookdale, and the success of his experiments on the smelting of iron with coke. The Quaker potters of Bristol, the brassfounders of Bristol and Birmingham, the ironmasters of Furness, and those of Sheffield (Fell and Milner), and the great group of ironmasters of South Wales, are all illustrative of this close attention to technical research. No doubt industry gained a great deal by the exclusion of Friends from the

Universities and from the learned professions, which must have released for industry the brains and energy that otherwise would have gone there. In addition, Friends' simplicity of life, their abstention from many of the social habits of their day, and their slight interest in the arts, music and literature, left them a large share of surplus energy for their businesses and for the service of Friends.

The early history of the London Lead Company in many ways emphasizes these points. The story is full of technical interest which would be out of place here, but it contains a surprising demonstration of widespread activity ranging over the whole of the British Isles, springing in the early part from the energies of a small handful of pioneers, nearly all members of the Society of Friends.

In a brief summary of that history, it is necessary to start with the Charter of the " Bristol Company ", although that was not acquired by Friends until 1704, because that is the Charter under which the London Lead Company carried out all its work. Lead mining has been carried on in Britain from pre-Roman times, being systematized by the Romans during the first century of our era. After the departure of the Romans, the mines were largely neglected until the monastic period, when lead was sought over most of the country, being in great demand for roofing and for pipes and cisterns for water supply. The monastic mining was usually short lived, and confined to surface and very shallow working. It was not until the sixteenth century, when many of the mines passed into lay hands at the dissolution of the monasteries, that systematic exploitation began. The first great mining venture of the new type was actually concerned with copper more than with lead, and was the venture, mainly by Germans, in the Lake District, under the charter of the Society of Mines Royal. Sir Humphrey Mackworth in the seventeenth century introduced systematic mining in Wales, but by the end of that century the whole industry was only just on the threshold of its main development. Lead had been smelted almost entirely with charcoal, and as most other metals were also worked in charcoal furnaces, a timber shortage was threatened throughout the country. This turned attention to the possibilities of smelting metals, using coal as a fuel and thus saving timber.

THE CHARTER OF THE GOVERNOR AND COMPANY

In 1692 a series of petitions were placed before William and Mary, asking for the incorporation of several royal chartered companies, to be concerned with mining,[1] the main petitioner being one Constantine Vernatty, supported by Thomas Addison, a man already concerned in the iron mining and smelting industry. Among these various petitions is one of March 12th, 1692, the parent of the Company we are studying :—

Proceedings upon the petition of Constantine Vernatty, Thomas Addison, and John Nix, esqs., John Moore and George Moore of London, Merchants. Shows that they have with several others at the expense of several thousand pounds, brought to perfection a very useful art or invention of smelting down lead ore, with pit and sea coal, and making the same into good and merchantable sheet lead, shot, bullets, and other lead, which has not so effectually been put into practice by any persons before. That in regard it requires a considerable stock for the improvement and carrying on the said undertaking, which cannot easily be raised, but by a joint stock and incorporation under the Great Seal, they pray her Majesty to incorporate them and such others as they shall nominate by the name of the *Governor and Company of Lead Miners in England and Wales*. Referred to the Attorney or Solicitor General. (S.P. Dom. Petition Entry Bk. 1.0.249.)

Following the consideration of this petition, several companies were incorporated as Company for Digging and Working of Mines, Company of Mine Adventurers, Company of Copper Miners in England, etc., and the one promoted by Vernatty finally incorporated as a smelting company on October 4th, 1692. On October 13th the promoters called a meeting of the proprietors, the minutes of this meeting being the first entry in the London Lead Company minute books, as follows (see Plate VI) :—

IN THE NAME OF ALMIGHTY GOD AMEN.
London Thursday the 13th October 1692
Att the halfe Moone Taverne In Cheapside.

Present

Messrs. Richard Owen Esqr Messrs. George Moore
       Francis Baker Esqr   Thomas Addison Esqr
       George Clerke Esqr   Constantine Vernatty Esqr
       John Franke   John Moore
       Richard Adams   John Henly

Messrs. Sr. Henry Marwood   Messrs. Francis Parry Esqr
William Moore   Thomas Renda
Thomas Nix   Joseph Gaithwaite
Richar Webster   William Maismore
William Perris

Their Majesties Charter for Incorporateing the Governour & Compa. for smelting downe of Lead with Pittcoale and Seaacoale dated the 4th of this Instant October In the 4th Yeare of their Reigne: was this day read and Thankefully accepted by the above Gentlemen.

AND That each pson may be capable to receive the benefitt of said Letters Pattents of Incorporation the above Gentlemen agreed that the following oath shall be taken by each Member In the words foll: Vizt.

I: A: B: doe sincerely Promise and Swear that I will be faithful to the Governour and Company for Smelting downe Lead with Pittcoale and Seacoale, the secretts of the said Company that shall be given mee in charge to conceale I will not disclose and during the Joynt stocke of the said Company I will not directly or indirectly by my selfe nor by or with any other Person or Company carry on or contribute towards the carrying on the Smelting downe of Lead with Pittcoale and Seacoale to the Prejudice of the Company within the Limitts of their Charter
                                Soe help me God.

AND Then the Gentlemen above named desired Richard Owen Esqr (nominated in the Charter to be the Present Governour) that he would please this night to take the oaths directed by the Charter with the aforegoeing oath before the Present Lord Mayor and that they would meete him att this place to morrow Morning att nine of the Clocke to receive said oaths from him that being qualified according as directed In said Letters Pattents they might proceed to the managemt. of the Companys affaires &c.

Memorandum that 10 of the Clocke att night Richard Owen Esqr Tooke ye oaths as appoynted by ye Charter; and another agreed to by this Compa. & being soe qualified commenced Govr. of this Corporation.

A meeting was held on Friday, October 14th, at which the members of the Court of Assistants were sworn, and it was appointed to meet on the Tuesday following at 4 p.m., after which they went to view apartments that were to let in Sadlers Hall, appointing Messrs. Renda and Moore to treat for the tenancy of these chambers as their offices. At the following meeting, more members of the Court were sworn, and a lengthy preamble to be subscribed by all members, regulating the terms of qualification for membership and for holding and surrendering shares, was agreed to.* The Company's capital was to be of 1,000 shares of £18 each, members of the Company to hold not less than ten shares. Richard Rickards was sworn Secretary and Richard Adams sworn Treasurer to the Company.

The Corporation so constituted by Charter was to be directed by a Governor and Court of twenty-four Assistants, with a Deputy Governor, all being elected annually at a General Meeting. The Court met every Tuesday in the year, and such other days each month as were necessary for discussion of business and special reports. This arrangement held good until the end of the Company in 1905.

At its meeting on October 19th, the Court of Assistants (referred to hereafter as the Court) was informed that Talbot Clerk (a patentee of the process of smelting lead with coal) had " a very convenient Lead Works all ready built fitt for the Immediate Smelting downe of Lead " with all tools, furnaces, stocks of materials, etc., at Bristol.² The Court agreed to pay Clerk £9,000 for his works, giving him credit in the Company's books for this amount, and the works became the property of the Company. The office remained in London with a manager and secretary at the Bristol works, who reported weekly and shipped all smelted lead to London for sale.

The works at Bristol began to smelt lead late in 1692, buying ore in miscellaneous lots from Sir Carberry Price and others in Wales and on the borders. Their methods of buying ore were not efficient, and their furnaces, smelting and refining processes were unsatisfactory. It is very clear from numerous reports that the claims made in their petition, of skill in smelting lead with coal, could not be substantiated ; there are frequent reports of ore spoiled in the smelting, refining furnaces not working properly, and their product being rejected in the open market. The agent at the Bristol works was accused of malpractices and bad management, and after investigation was dismissed. The difficulties of the

* The Charter with comments appears in *Trans.* Selden Soc., v, 28, 1913, pp. 228-30, and Pat. Rolls 4 Wm. Mary, pt. vii. The Charter and preamble are printed in " London Lead Company " (Raistrick), *Trans.* Newcomen Soc., xiv, 1934, pp. 119-62.

Company accumulated, and after visits and inspections by several of the Court members a recommendation to close the venture was made and accepted at a General Meeting on May 27th, 1695. The Company handed back the works to Talbot Clerk, who, however, failed to make any further use of them, nor did he make any progress with his smelting methods.[3] After nine years' inactivity the Company was acquired by a number of members of the Society of Friends, and the charter became the foundation of the Quaker Lead Company.

Of the promoters of the charter under which the Bristol Company worked, several were already interested in both lead and iron smelting, but they had been prevented from operating their lead smelting processes by the existence of a patent granted in 1678 to Grandison. Talbot Clerk's Bristol works had been built by his father, Sir Clement Clerk, but were closed in 1686 following a patent infringement decision of the Privy Council. The expiry of Grandison's patent in 1692 gave Clerk and the others the chance they wanted to secure their own charter, and it was probably a matter of policy that kept Clerk's name out of the petitions and dictated the peculiar method of taking over his works.[4] The existence of Grandison's patent until 1692 and then the charter of the Governor and Company, in the following years, were blocking the work of Dr. Edward Wright and other Friends who had made considerable experiments and improvements in lead and copper smelting, and in the construction of furnaces; consequently, before this Quaker group could develop its new furnaces and methods of production, they must secure the transfer of the charter to their own Company. How this was accomplished we shall see later.

The early work of Wright is unfortunately almost unknown, but from 1697 is fairly well documented in the minute books of the Royal Mines Copper and the London Lead Company.** The first minute in the remaining minute book of the Royal Mines Copper (hereafter referred to as the Welsh Company) is taken at a meeting at Vernon's Coffee House, London, November 30th, 1697—present Dr. Edward Wright,* chairman, Thomas Cooper,* Peter de Lannoy,* Samuel Davies, Richard Matthews and Captain

* Then or later (before 1704) members of the Society of Friends.

** minute book of the Royal Mines Copper for 1692-7 is now known.

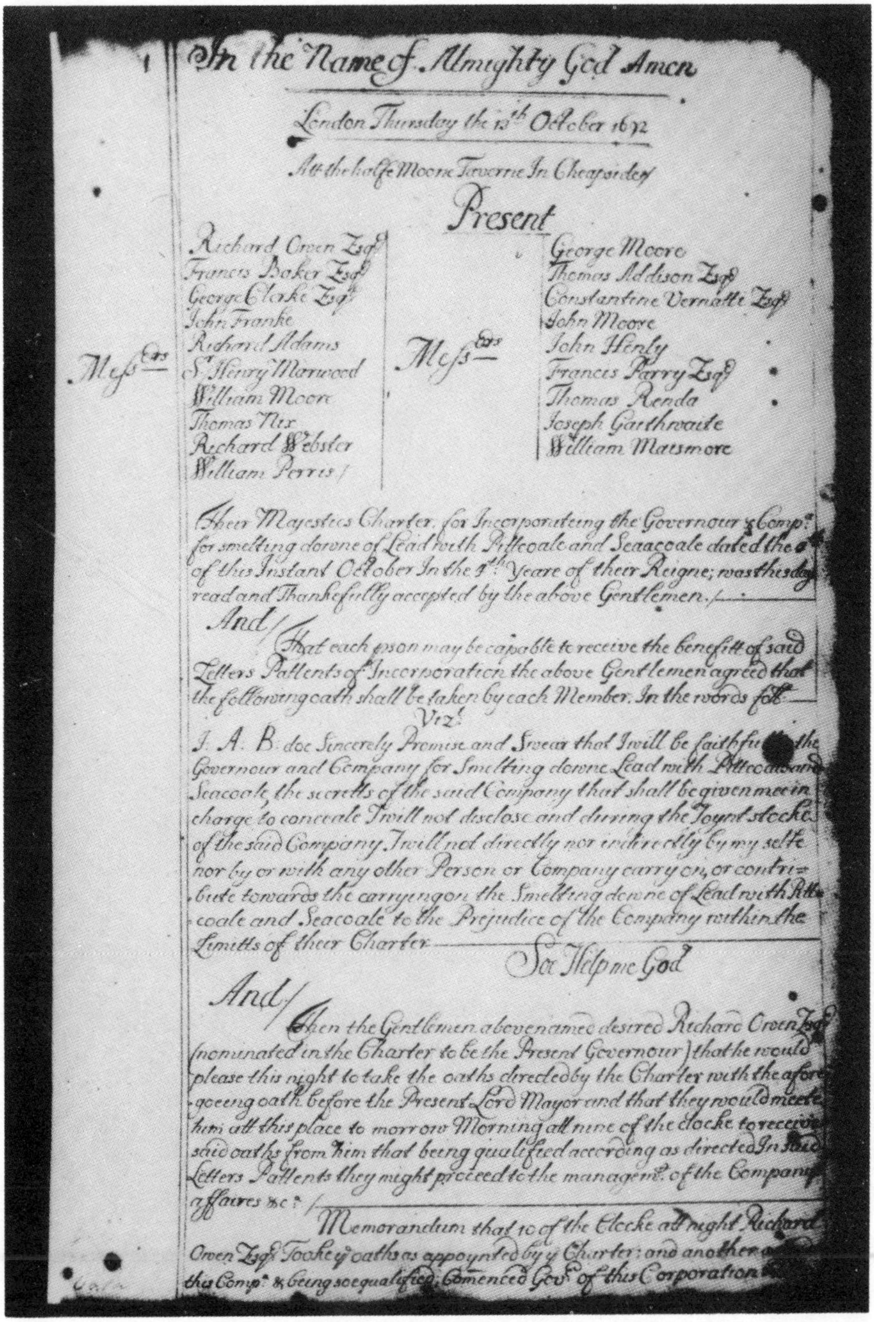

In the Name of Almighty God Amen

London Thursday the 13th October 1692

At the halfe Moone Taverne In Cheapside

Present

Messrs
- Richard Owen Esqr
- Francis Baker Esqr
- George Clarke Esqr
- John Franke
- Richard Adams
- Sr Henry Marwood
- William Moore
- Thomas Nix
- Richard Webster
- William Perris

Messrs
- George Moore
- Thomas Addison Esqr
- Constantine Vernatti Esqr
- John Moore
- John Henry
- Francis Parry Esqr
- Thomas Renda
- Joseph Garthwaite
- William Matsmore

Their Majesties Charter, for Incorporateing the Governour & Compa: for smelting downe of Lead with Pittcoale and Seacoale dated the 6 of this Instant October In the 4th yeare of their Reigne; was this day read and Thankefully accepted by the above Gentlemen.

And That each pson may be capable to receive the benefitt of said Letters Pattents of Incorporation the above Gentlemen agreed that the following oath shall be taken by each Member. In the words foll:

Vizt.

I. A. B. doe sincerely Promise and Sweare that I will be faithfull to the Governour and Company for Smelting downe Lead with Pittcoale and Seacoale, the secrets of the said Company that shall be given mee in charge to conceale I will not disclose and dureing the Joynt stocke of the said Company, I will not directly nor indirectly by my selfe nor by or with any other Person or Company carry on, or contribute towards the carryingon the Smelting downe of Lead with Pittcoale and Seacoale to the Prejudice of the Company within the Limitts of their Charter

So Help me God

And Then the Gentlemen abovenamed desired Richard Owen Esqr (nominated in the Charter to be the Present Governour) that he would please this night to take the oaths directed by the Charter with the aforegoeing oath before the Present Lord Mayor and that they would meete him att this place to morrow Morning att nine of the clocke to receive said oaths from him that being qualified according as directed In said Letters Pattents they might proceed to the management of the Companys affaires &c.

Memorandum that 10 of the Clocke att night Richard Owen Esqr Tooke ye oaths as appointed by ye Charter and another of this Compa: & being soe qualified, Comenced Govr of this Corporation

Plate IX First page of the first minute book, 1692, entitled "Fair Minute Book of the London Lead Company."

Plate X Entrance to the Haggs Level, Nentsberry Mine, Alston.

Plate XI Remains of a waterwheel and ore crushers at St John's Mine, upper South Tyne Valley.

William Thompson. The Royal Mines Copper are vested in Wm. Monsen esqr., Wm. Thompson esqr. and John Linton, Gent., as Trustees, at that time, but later passed into the hands of the Company. The Company had existed for several years, as this book refers back to earlier minute books, and some of its earliest minutes refer to the winding up of old ventures in the North.

The Company had been concerned in copper mines in Cumberland, Westmorland, and Lancashire, mainly at Caldbeck, Keswick and Coniston (the sites of the mines held by the German miners under a charter of Elizabeth) and also in Wales.5 The Germans, after more than a century of active mining, had been expelled from the mines and much of their work destroyed, largely as a result of political intrigue in which they had no part. How the Friends, Edward Wright, John Haddon and Thomas Cooper, acquired the concessions the Germans had held is still a mystery. In addition to the copper, they were mining some quantity of lead at various places in the Lake District, and making iron at Hackett Forge, Little Langdale.* In addition to these northern sites, there was close connection with the Mine Adventurers of Wales, to whom they sold some of the surplus ore from their mines in Flintshire. Wright is described as "physician at the sign of the Ship, neare the Monument in London ", and was associated possibly with the invention, and certainly with the improvement, of the reverberatory furnace.† During the period of the Welsh Company he was experimenting both there and in the North, in the application of his furnace to the smelting of lead, and also in a process for the extraction of silver from silver-lead ores, but as his methods became sufficiently successful for the production of both silver and lead on a commercial scale, he found his way blocked by the charter already held by the Bristol Company. In 1692 or later, Wright, Cooper and Haddon of the Welsh Company were associated in the formation of the " Ryton Company " at Newcastle-on-Tyne. The early history of this company is still very obscure but should be of outstanding interest to Friends. From a list

* Cal. State Papers, Dom. 1692, and Raistrick, *Trans*. Newcomen Soc., xiv, 1934, p. 128.
† Schluter, *Grundliche Unterricht von Huttewerken*, etc., 1738, p. 110 ; Raistrick, Lead Mining and Smelting in N. Pennines, *Univ. Durham Phil. Soc.*, ix, 1936.

of books belonging to the London Lead Company, copied into their minute book, it is clear that the Ryton Company was formed prior to 1696, and in 1697 it was buying lead ore in Alderstane (Alston) Moor, and smelting it and extracting silver, at its works at Ryton-on-Tyne. Most of the shareholders were presumably Friends, as on incorporation with the London Lead Company in 1704 most took affirmation in lieu of oath in proclaiming their allegiance to the charter. The works of the Company were in Ryton parish, west of Newcastle, on the site of the present railway station at Blaydon. Ore was purchased at various mines both in Alston Moor and around Blanchland in the Derwent valley (the tributary to the Tyne at Blaydon), and sundry packets of ore were sent by Wright from Caldbeck, Cumberland. There was a very close connection between the Welsh Company and the Ryton group, not only through Wright, Haddon and Cooper, but through other shareholders in common, and the minutes of the Royal Mines Copper include frequent notes of apparatus sent from Wales to Ryton and notes on certain trials of ore and processes there. Between 1696 and 1704 the Ryton Company bought certain mines near Alston,* while the Welsh Company had numerous leases of mines in Flintshire and other parts of Wales.

By 1701 the Welsh Company had closed down all their leases in the Lake District and were confining their activities to Wales, where their agent, Anthony Barker, was advised to look out for a suitable site for a " Cupola " (a smelt mill equipped with reverberatory furnaces). The local smelters and Mr. Peck, the mining agent for Mr. Mostyn of Halkyn, Flintshire, strongly advised Barker to stick to the old and well-tried " blast " furnace or " hearth ", but Wright persisted in his faith in the new reverberatory or " cupola ". The Company, not finding a " mill " to lease, decided in 1702 to build their own, and in 1703 secured a site for purchase at Gadlis, Bagilt, near Flint. A smelting house with four furnaces for smelting lead ore, a refining furnace for silver, and a slag hearth were built, and later houses, workshops, stores, etc., added. The site can be seen close to the railway side, just as Bagilt station on the Chester-Rhyl

---

* Tyne Green, Windy Brae, Clargill and others in Tyne Head, near the source of the South Tyne, and a share in Blaegill in the Nent valley, a tributary of the South Tyne. (See Plate VII.)

line is approached from the east. This site was conveniently near the many leases the Company had taken up in the Halkyn mountain district, and also close to the Mostyn collieries for coal and the Dee for shipping facilities. Development at Ryton kept pace with this, but licence to smelt lead in the reverberatory furnace, using coal, could not be obtained because of the already existing charter held by the relict of the Bristol Company.

Edward Wright and Enoch Ffloyd were commissioned to explore ways and means of obtaining the transfer to the Welsh Company of the charter of the Governor and Company, and early in 1704 reported that a way had been found. The only way open was for some of their members to become members of the Governor and Company by purchase of shares, and to fill up the Court of Assistants in the same way. There was, however, a serious difficulty in this, as all members of the Governor and Company, on election, had to take an oath of allegiance as appointed by the charter. On February 10th, 1704, a General Court of the Governor and Company was called by the surviving Deputy Governor, Thomas Addison, and was attended by only three other survivors of the old Court. Their first business was to admit as members of the Company and then elect to the Court, seven non-Friends from the Welsh Company, who could take the oaths required. Samuel Davies (of the Welsh Company) was elected the Governor, and it was reported that the shares of the old Company were to be sold at 2s. each.[6] At the next meeting three days later, the old preamble was revised and certain articles annulled, then Davies reported that :—

Sir Symon Harcourt (Solicitor General) agrees that affirmation of a Quaker is admissible in place of the oaths for entry into the Company.

After a short discussion, the minutes proceed :—

Agreed/ . . . . to admit Quakers to any office in the Court and Company.

Edward Wright, Cornelius Mason, John Haddon, Jacob Franklin, and Thomas Cooper took the affirmation in lieu of oaths and were admitted to the Company.

Thomas Addison, Sir Hy. Marwood, Thos. Renda, Capt. Thos. Nix, and John Henly did, immediately after the last general Court sell out all shares, hence they forfeit all offices.

Also/ . . . . Sir Talbot Clerk, Rich. Adams, Geo. Moore, and Matthias Cupper sold out and forfeited all offices.

Also/ . . . . Fr. Scobell, Hy. Tate, and Gabriel Glover failed to take oath so are not members.

Proceeded to elect Depty. Governor Enoch Ffloyd and five assistants.

Dr. Ed. Wright, Cornelius Mason, John Haddon, Jacob Franklin, Thos. Cooper.

In these two meetings we see, nine years after the winding up of the Bristol venture, the Governor and Company for Smelting downe Lead with Pittcoale and Seacoale come into new life, and by a regular procedure effect a complete change of personnel, the early promoters selling out their shares after holding office long enough to elect a new group on to the Court of the Company. This small group all take oaths, but immediately after announce the legality of the affirmation for Quakers, a question that must have taken a long time of enquiry and preparation. This granted, a group of Quakers then join the Company and the handful of original promoters, who have carried through the transfer, gracefully retire, leaving an entirely new body of people invested with the whole powers and privileges of the original charter. The affirmation is perhaps of interest, if only for its extraordinary language and its very slight variance from the oath :—

THE AFFIRMATION taken by the Members of the Corporation of the Governor and Company for Smelting down LEAD &c. appointed by their CHARTER.

I, A.... B.... do solemnly and sincerely promise and declare, that I will be true and faithfull to King GEORGE ; and do solemnly, sincerely, and truely profess, testify, and declare, that I do from my heart abhor, detest, and renounce, as impious and heretical, that wicked Doctrine and Position, That Princes excommunicated or deprived by the POPE, or any Authority of the See of Rome, may be deposed or murthered by their Subjects, or any other whatsoever.

AND I do declare, that no foreign Prince, Person, Prelate, State or Potentate, hath, or ought to have, any Power, Jurisdiction, Superiority, Preeminence, or Authority, Ecclesiastical or Spiritual within this Realm.

AND further I do solemnly declare, that I will be true and faithfull to the Governor and Company for smelting down Lead with Pit-Coal and Sea-Coal, during my continuance in the said Joint-Stock.

In the form of oath, the differences are slight. A.... B.... promises and *swears*, *abjures* instead of renounces the *damnable* instead of wicked doctrine of the first paragraph, and adds at the end of all, So help me GOD.

THE QUAKER LEAD COMPANY, 1704-30

With the completion of the transfer just described, the leading members of the Welsh Company were invested with the charter for smelting lead, etc., in due form of law, and

Fig 5   The arms of the London Lead Company.

could proceed at once to business. Most of the Quaker members of the Welsh Company were also members of the entirely Quaker Ryton Company, and a fusion of the two companies under the newly-acquired charter produced the " Quaker Lead Company " or " London Lead Company ", neither of these being official titles, but both being quickly adopted for general use and convenience, in place of the cumbersome title of the Governor and Company, etc., etc. The procedure to obtain the fusion was fairly simple. At a meeting of the Court on February 27th, 1704–5, the Court was " informed " of rich lead mines in Flintshire, with a cupola, furnaces, refinery, tools, stock, workmen, and a handsome dwelling house, buildings, etc., leased for " near 40 years to come ".

There is a stock of 700 shares, about 8% per annum, for interest, and it amounts to near £50 a share. . . .

Recommended that £50 a share be raised on each of these shares and that members may transfer one or more shares in Royal Mines Copper in lieu and in full payment for the new £50 shares, etc.

On May 15th, 1705, the same procedure was adopted for the transfer of shares in the Ryton Company, these being valued for surrender or exchange at £125. The whole stock of both Companies was tendered, so that by July 1705, Ryton and Gadlis smelt mills and the mines in Alston Moor and Flintshire were part of the new Company, the Governor and Company for Smelting down Lead with Pit Coal and Sea Coal, usually known as the London Lead Company.

By July 1705, both smelt mills, Ryton and Gadlis, were in full work, and cakes of silver and pigs of lead were being shipped from Newcastle-on-Tyne and from the Dee, to London, the silver being delivered into the Mint in cakes, there cast into ingots after assay, and the value of each ingot returned to the Treasurer of the Company.[7] It is interesting to find that, without exception, the value of the silver is returned along with a large extra payment, as the silver proved on assay to be finer than the standard silver of the Mint. In the earlier minutes of the Royal Mines Copper, it is noted time after time that Wright is able to refine a better silver and extract more silver from any parcel of lead, than any other smelter in the country, and throughout its history the London Lead Company maintained this tradition of superiority in silver extraction and refining.

The reason that the London Lead Company developed as a large silver refining corporation is not perhaps clear to the lay reader, unfamiliar with the mineralogy and metallurgy of lead. Practically all the richest deposits of lead ores in this country are vein deposits, in which the lead occurs in the form of lead sulphide, the mineral galena. Almost all galena contains some silver, and although this does not often amount to more than $\frac{1}{20}$ per cent., the mineral is one of the

THE "QUAKER LEAD COMPANY"

most profitable ores of silver. The silver cannot be separated by mechanical means, as the silver can almost be regarded as being in solution in the lead. The silver content of galena is generally measured by the number of ounces of silver troy measure contained in a ton avoirdupois of the smelted lead. The richest ore that the London Lead Company smelted from its northern area was that from the Clargill vein near Tyne Head, which is reported as having upwards of 36 oz. of silver per ton of lead. Some of the other rich veins carried 12 to 16 oz. per ton, while the general average over all their mines was nearer 8 oz. per ton, and occasionally in particular veins was as low as 4 or 5 oz. per ton. The smelted lead contained the silver in solution, and the process of "refining" was adapted to recover the silver with the minimum loss of lead in the process. This was necessary not only because of the value of the silver, but because the presence of even a small quantity of silver in the lead was apt to make it brittle and very unsuited for many industrial purposes.

The lead to be refined is melted in a reverberatory furnace, on a bed or "test" made up on the furnace bottom, of bone ashes—that is, finely-ground calcined bones. With skilled regulation of the temperature and furnace flames, the lead is melted, then oxidized to the yellow oxide litharge, and the litharge becomes molten. The temperature at which the litharge melts is too low for the silver to be oxidized and so the silver remains in the metallic state. Much of the molten litharge can be drawn off from the furnace bottom, and the "test" of bone ash absorbs all the litharge that remains, without being corroded by it as stone or brick would be. On completion of the process, all the lead has been changed to litharge and either run off or absorbed into the test, leaving the silver as an isolated cake in the furnace. The silver cakes are then remelted and cast in ingots, while the litharge and the test with its charge of absorbed litharge are returned to a reducing furnace and resmelted to metallic lead. The loss of lead in the process is comparatively small when the furnace is well designed and used with skill. It was in the design of the furnace and the details of the process that the Company soon excelled all its rivals and secured the first position in the country as silver refiners. The London Lead Company soon found that the bone ashes they were buying in London and shipping to Gadlis and Ryton were not sufficiently pure for their purposes, so commenced to make their own. After a short time they made the curious discovery that if the bone ashes in the test were mixed with stale beer they were very much improved in quality, and they sanctioned the addition of a small brew house to the furnace plant for this purpose of providing beer for the bone ashes. On some occasions the Company considered whether or not it would be more profitable to sell their litharge to the glass makers rather than reduce it back to lead, but after some time they found it more economical to reduce to lead.

This separation of silver by " cupellation ", as the above process is called, was only changed in 1833 when Pattinson, who was born in Alston and was smelter for Mr. Beaumont at the Ryton smelt mill (sold to Beaumont by the London Lead Company), discovered his method of crystallization. In that process, the silver-rich lead was melted in a series of set pans each kept at a critical temperature by a small fire under it, and kept for some time at the right temperature. On cooling gradually, crystals of lead begin to form in the liquid metal, and Pattinson found by analysis that this crop of first crystals was considerably poorer in silver than the original melt, and the liquid remaining was enriched. By repetition of the process several times, the silver-rich liquid being time after time recrystallized, the silver is concentrated into a small amount of rich alloy and most of the lead desilverized was rendered very pure. This process effected very considerable saving in fuel and cut down considerably the loss of lead, with the result that much poorer silver lead could be refined by this process than by cupellation. The old process was able to refine lead with about 6 oz. of silver, and make it pay, but with the Pattinson process 2 or 3 oz. lead could be refined economically.

Pattinson's process was patented in 1833 and the Company were quick to give it a trial. The first trials were made at Nent Head, where a set of " crystallizing pans " was built in the old smelt mill. The progress of the experiment can be traced in the following very terse minutes :—

1836   Pattinson's Patent for refining lead by crystalisation has been tried. The right to use the process to be purchased for £1,050.

1837   Great advantage of Refining by Cristalisation noted. The loss of lead by the process is only equal to 1/373 rd part of the lead used.
Considerable improvements in the process have been made by Mr. Stagg (the Company's agent) and experiments with his improvements are highly satisfactory though requiring changes in the mode of conducting the process.
Conditional agreement to purchase the patent completed.
1839   Crystalisation process improved by Mr. Stagg's invention for saving much of the labour.
1840, -41, and -42, further reports of great improvements made in the process.

Some of Stagg's improvements were embodied in further patents, Stagg maintaining friendly relations and correspondence with Pattinson all the time. The improved crystallization method was adopted at Stanhope, Bollihope, Eggleston and Nent Head mills, and remained in use until the end of the Company.

Throughout the early years of the London Lead Company (1705-37) the Company sent all its silver to the Mint, where it was used in the redemption of the coinage, in consideration of which the Court in December 1705 petitioned the Crown for a device to be stamped on all coinage minted from the Company's silver. The suggested device is given in the following minute :—

That inasmuch as this Corporation doth make silver both in England & Wales, the Lord High Treasurer be petitioned for Two Roses & Two Feathers Quartered as the Emblems of Eng. & Wales.

Sir Isaac Newton, then Master of the Mint, took up the question with the Treasury, and after some delays (such as " the Lord High Treasurer is gone to New Market without ordering the warrant ", etc.) in 1706 the Queen gave a warrant for such a device, renewing the warrant in 1709 as follows :—

18th Jan. 1709.
The Treasurer reported that the warrant for the distinction of the Company's coin is ready.

ANNE R.
WHEREAS our High Treasurer of England hath laid before us as well the petition of ye Governor and Company for Smelting down

lead with pit coal and sea coal praying for their encouragement that we would be graciously pleased to direct you the Master and worker of our Mint to coyn such silver as they shall produce from such lead with the mark of distinction affixed to their said petition as also the report made by you and the rest of the principall officers of our Mint thereupon and we graciously being pleased to gratifie the petitioners in their said request our will and pleasure is and we do hereby will and direct authorise and comand that all such silver as shall be brought into our said Mint extracted from lead by the aforesaid art of smelting and refining be from time to time coyned with all convenient speed into the current coyns of this our realm with the mark of distinction on each respective piece as in the form requested in the draught to their petition hereunto annexed and for so doing this shall be your warrant given at our court in St. James the 20th day of Aprill in the fifth year of our reigne
by her Majesties command
Godolphin
To our Trusty and Wellbeloved Sr. Isaac Newton Knt.
Master and worker of our Mint.

ANNE R.
Whereas the Gov. and Company for smelting downe lead with pit cole and sea cole have humbly besought us upon the occasion of the Union to renew the directions we gave by our warrant bearing date the 10th Aprill 1706 in the 5th year of our Reign for coyning such silver as they shall extract from such lead with the mark of distinction depicted in the margeant—and we being graciously pleased to condescend to their request, . . . etc.

The former warrant is here repeated and sent to Newton at the Mint.

The " device " suggested appeared on most of the issue of 5s., 2s. 6d., 1s. and 6d. pieces minted between 1706 and 1737, i.e. on coins of Anne, George I and George II. (See Plate VIII.) Although the meaning of this " device " was in recent years almost forgotten, a few people still knew the coins that bore it as "Quaker shillings", and Pennant in his history of Holywell, 1796, remarks upon them with a note that during the period of the Company in Gadlis (1704-90) they provided from Wales alone 430,604 oz. of pure silver. With the production at Ryton and other mills in the North, we can estimate that in the first forty years of its history the Company produced over one million ounces of silver (at its highest production, 1830-70, it produced over 2½ million ounces). In 1737 as the Company were selling silver to the Mint at less than current market price, they had an expert re-examination of the charter, and decided that if they so desired they were entirely free to sell their silver in the open market. In 1766 the Solicitors of the Mint claimed that the Company were bound to send in silver to the Mint as required, but the Company stuck to their decision that nothing in their charter, nor in the Act of 1st William and Mary, Cap. 30, obliged them to sell their silver at 5s. 2d. per ounce, which was Mint price, if they wished to get a better price elsewhere. After much correspondence and inspection of the charter, this view was accepted by the Solicitor to the Mint. Since 1737, however, and for long after 1766, the Quaker silver was still bought by the Mint for coining the Maunday money.

With the success of Ryton and Gadlis, the Company began to seek new sources of silver-rich lead ores, preferring where possible to lease and work the actual mines, rather than purchase ore in the market. It was a policy that made them essentially a mining corporation throughout their history, although their charter was only concerned with the smelting side of their business.

The method of following out this policy was fairly simple. Edward Wright, Samuel Davies and John Haddon, with occasionally Urban Hall and other members of the Court, were instructed or requested by the Court to make frequent tours of inspection of all the Company's "works" and to report thereon, and to visit and consult with the district agents, Anthony Barker in Wales and Thomas Allsopp in the North. On these tours the various lead markets were visited en route, and where the men heard of or saw good ore for sale they usually arranged to visit the mines producing it. In this way they " heard of " the mines around Blanchland in the Derwent valley, of Teesdale, Wanlock Head and Stirling in Scotland, of the Orkneys, Isle of Man, Mendips, Derbyshire, and Southern Ireland. All these places in turn were visited, ores sampled and sent to the mills at Gadlis or in the North for trial, and eventually leases taken of some of the mines. When one remembers that the land journeys were performed on horseback, and that the mining districts were all remote and mountainous, we must have great respect for the courage and endurance of all these pioneers. There is not much reference to the actual incidents of travel, but we do get occasional glimpses of their adventures as in a visit to the North (Alston Moor) in 1706 :—

All on horseback, . . . tis to be remarked that in this Country tis the most troublesome and dangerous riding of any part of England, being extremely hilly, stony, and boggy. There is no travelling but with a guide, nor then, but in danger of Horse and Man.

Somewhat similar comments occur about the journey from Wales, through Derbyshire to Alston Moor, and from Edinburgh to Wanlock Head. The London to Edinburgh journey was occasionally taken by sea.

In the various minutes relating to shipment of lead and silver from Wales, there are reports of shipwreck and attempted salvage on the wild coasts of Pembroke and Gower, and of piracy, the failure of convoys, chases by French privateers, as thrilling and hair-raising as anyone could desire.

In the early part of 1703 when the works in Wales were well under way and were producing a fair quantity of lead, Edward Wright was commissioned by the Court to report on the best arrangements that could be entered into for the transport of the smelted lead to London. In April he reported that " ye best way seems to be by getting Lead from Flint to any of the Welch Collieries that serves Plymouth with Coles and so from Plymouth to London ". On May 4th a letter from him states :—

That we have discoursed Walter Benthall about contracting with Henry Mason Mr. of ye Edward and Sarah burthen 70 tunns or thereabouts to goe from Plymouth to Fflint, there to load with lead and from thence to London with Convoy at 46s. p. hundred pieces of 21 pces to ye tunn and 6 score to ye Piece with 2/3 rds Port Charges and primage and average as accustomed whch ye Cttee doe approve of and ye said Dr. Wright and Mr. Haddon is hereby desired to and Ordered to enter into Charter party with ye sd Mr accordingley.

May 11th. Wrote to Anth. Barker to freight a vessel or two there (i.e. at Chester or Flint) and load them with lead to Milford for ye Loyal Cook from ye East Indies now lies, in order to come to London under her convoy.

Several similar items follow, then :—

June 29th. A letter read from John Booker datd 25th Inst. that he was safe arrived in ye Downes and that he designed to proceed to ye westward with Convoy.

July 13th. That Mr. Tho. Cooper make assurance upon ye first notice of ye Shipps being arrived at Fflint, vizt. £400 on ye Owners Adventure John Booker Master and £500 on ye Penelope, Lyon Mr. from thence to London on ye best terms he can with Convoy.

Aug. 17th. Reports that assurance made of £500 on ye Penelope at 4 guineas p.C. from Darpoole to London, warrant with Convoy and the same for Owners Adventure.

Aug. 31st. Dr. Wright reports that he has spoke to Adam Axnet mr. of the Primrose, in which ye 20 odd Tunns of Lead is mencioned to be aboard him in ye minute of ye 1 June last, from Wales to London, who told ye said Dr. Wright that coming out of Bleau Morris with another small vessell in Company ye Convoy being at some distance before them, they spied a small sail making towards them wch supposed to be English, haveing English Colours flying, but after coming near each other and haling she proved to be a French Privateer wch boarding ye said Primrose, they carried her into France—the Insurance made by Mr. Cooper on ye Owners Adventure and ye Penelope being made from Chester Water to London with Convoy and there being no Convoy to be had from Chester Water to Dublin, Ordered . . . proper assurance be made on best terms.

Sept. 21st. letter from J. Booker at Dublin sailing for London under Convoy of Man of Warr called ye Feversham.

Oct. 12th. letter from J.B. at Milford ye 4th inst. with advice of his being safe arrived there from Dublin without Convoy but that he waited there to depart, under ye Convoy of the Dolphin Man of Warr and Hastings.

Dec. 4th. Letter read from John Booker giving an Account of a disaster by the late Stormes whereby his Shipp was put ashore and damaged so that ye Lead on board must bee unshipt. Agreed that a letter be writ to Alderman John Rixon of Pembroke to take care of the goods and make report to us as soon as possible what condition the Shipp is in and in case of need to advance 20 or 30 lbs. on Bottomree Bond for the dispatch of ye sd Shipp wch was done accordingly.

Jan. 25th, 1704. A letter was read from John Booker dated ye 15th Inst. at Milford aquainting that being very much in distress for want of money in fitting up his shipp, provisions, etc., he had sold 1 Tunn of Lead to Alderman Rixon of Pembroke at £9 pr H.pcs 120 lbs. to ye pc. also that he had disposed of 2 Tunns more at £8 10s. p.H.pc, in all £26—That his vesell was tight and well and that he was making the best of his way for London, butt by stress of Weather was forced into Milford from whence he assigned to proceed on his voyage with ye first opportunity.

Feb. 1. It being proposed to some of this Cttee by Mr. Richd. Diamond that there is a small vessell formerly a french Privateer will bee sold cheap and may be fitt for ye Company's service to Transport their Lead from Wales to London or otherwise, it is Resolved that Dr. Wright, Mr. Haddon, Mr. Thos. Cooper and Mr. Mason be appointed to treat about it and buy ye same on the best terms they can if they see convenient.

Actual confirmation of this purchase is not recorded in the minutes, but later reports notice the quicker and safer journeys between Wales and London, and occasional successful escapes from privateers suggest that their ex-privateer was indeed a quick sailer and saved their lead on more than one occasion. Similar minutes re transport could be multiplied enormously, but the above will suffice to illustrate some of the difficulties encountered.

This first period of the Company drew towards a close in the later 1720's when Wright, Haddon and Davies were old men, when supervision of the rapidly increasing ventures over the whole of the British Isles was becoming impossible for them, and when their place on the Court was being taken by newer blood, including rather a heavy strain of purely business, non-Friend, speculators. The death of Wright in 1728, and most of the other promoters in the same decade, caused a great change in the policy of the Company. Although the Quaker tradition was strong enough to guide the Company in its relations with its workpeople, there was a short period following Wright's death when the Company counted only a minority of Friends in its Court. After some years, however, the Friends again came into a majority and by 1750 the Company was firmly established once more as the " Quaker Company ".

The smelt mill built at Gadlis continued as the centre of all the Welsh activities until the final closing down in that country, about 1790, a run of ninety-eight years in the one locality.[8] The mines which at first were rather widely scattered in Denbighshire, Merionethshire and Cardiganshire, were gradually given up, and equivalent leases concentrated in the Halkyn district, so that by 1730 the concern was nicely compacted within about thirty miles of the smelt mill. The principal leases were obtained from Mr. Mostyn of Halkyn, along with a small colliery leased near Gadlis, from Mr. Pennant, and to the end of their occupation Mostyn and Pennant remained good friends of the concern. The colliery provided all the coal for use in the smelt mill and refining houses, and also the coal for the domestic needs of the workmen. In connection with the transport of the smelted lead to London, the early practice had been to send the lead in small barges up the Dee, to meet the cheese boats sailing from Chester to London, and to load in mid-stream after due Customs examination. In 1733 a Bill was promoted in Parliament by the Chester merchants, for making a navigable channel up the Dee with quays and proper harbourage for large boats at Chester. The Company opposed this Bill on the grounds that " Lead, Litharge, etc., are now carried from Bagilt Mark to Parkgate, and there can be shipt as ballast in the Cheese ships. Distance is now 3 miles and freight at present is 1/6d. per ton. If the river is made navigable the Cheese ships will go right up to Chester and our lead will have to be carried 12 miles instead of three, before loading, as well as more dues payable to undertakers." The Bill, in spite of the opposition, was passed, but the Company obtained exemption from any additional river or loading dues that might be imposed by the operation of the Bill. Following this, the Company built a proper wharf at Bagilt shore, near to the smelt mill, and developed their own shipping direct from Bagilt to London.

Most of the reports of the Welsh area during the earlier years are almost entirely technical, as the smelters were very much concerned to improve all their processes. We do find incidental notes, however, from time to time that indicate good relations with the workmen and with the neighbourhood. The smelt mill was extended on several occasions, and houses added to the estate for the workmen. Much of the work at the mines was let out on " bargains ", the men prosecuting the bargain in their own way, the Company buying all the ore produced. A report in 1706 says :—

We found four furnaces at work, a slag hearth, and two refining furnaces. The refining keeps pace with the smelting. We advised Barker (the agent at Gadlis) to buy and always maintain large stocks of ore, to stabilise the price and to keep the works full. The Company can carry their trade to what degree they please. The Works are in splendid condition, and more efficient than anyone else's.

The works referred to were a block and two wings of buildings facing a large yard in which were situated store places for ore and lead, storehouses, offices, and the smelters' houses, blacksmith's shop and wood yard. The furnace house was 34 yards by 8 yards, brick built and slated, with two wings each 14 yards by 8 yards, one for slag hearth working and one for silver refining. The chimneys are noted as being much higher than the roof, with consequent good draught and ventilation. In 1729 the deputation note :—

All well at Gadlis though the country not being quite so honest as formerly, they are building a brick wall behind the workhouse (furnace and refinery) to inclose a yard for securing ye coales etc.

The Company were the earliest of the lead miners to adopt the steam engine for pumping, and in 1730 they bought second hand the famous Newcomen engine from York Buildings, London, and also ordered from the makers four other steam pumping engines for their Welsh mines.* As the mines were pursued to greater depths, considerable trouble was experienced in keeping them free from water, and before long the Company were forced to commence a deep drainage tunnel to unwater their area.

In 1722 the search for silver-rich ore which could be purchased to be refined in Wales, had led the Company's agents to Dublin, where they heard of and investigated a number of mines in south Ireland, in counties Cork and Tipperary, and eventually took a lease of them along with a smelt mill and sheet lead plant, in partnership with Richard Champion of Bristol two-sixteenths, James Griffiths of Swansea two-sixteenths and Edward Fenn of Cork one-sixteenth, the Company retaining eleven-sixteenths. The smelt mill was redesigned, the plant for sheet and pipe

---

* 3rd Oct. 1733. Have leased a great Coalwork on Dee, $\frac{1}{2}$ mls. from Gadlis, in which is a 5, 3, and 2 yd. coal seam sufficient for the works at Gadlis and all our engines. Ordered a Fire Engine of 33" Cyl. for £700 and are erecting another of 38" Cyl. and one of 35" Cyl. at Maeslogan. 6th May, 1731. Ordered a Fire Engine for Trelogan Mine 24" Cyl. 14th Sept., 1731. £105 licence paid for Fire Engine, paid Ezekial Trengrove. "Fire Engine" means a steam engine.

lead put in better order, and the site at Kilboy made the Irish headquarters. The venture proved a source of trouble from its remoteness and the difficulty of supervision. An early report says :—

Irish mines suffer under a weak manager who has allowed a Tippling House keeper to get control and to give absurd wages for poor work. . . . All improvements are opposed except in shot making. The mines are not so good as represented but still have good prospects.

The mining was carried on unwisely and by old and inefficient methods, and finally, lead manufacturers increasingly objected to the Company's activity in making sheet and pipes, as being outside the terms of their charter. This accumulation of difficulties led the Company to sell all their Irish ventures in 1741. The question of sheet and pipe making was raised again in 1810 and the Company took counsel's opinion on the matter, and the decision was that under the terms of their charter they certainly had no rights other than for smelting and refining lead.

In 1728 a small group of mines at Anglezarke, in the old parish of Bolton, Lancashire, were leased from Sir Thomas Standish for thirty-one years, and though they never became a great concern, they paid their way and, after the Company surrendered the lease, were reopened by later venturers and have produced a fair quantity of ore. These mines, small as they are, have considerable geological interest as being the first locality in which the mineral witherite,* carbonate of barium, was discovered and identified.

In 1720 the Company, through its agent, Anthony Barker, had tried several ores from Derbyshire, and instructed its representatives to explore the possibility and cost of obtaining leases of some of the mines from which the samples had come. Edward Wright and others interviewed Friends in the area, and eventually were put in contact with a man, George Graves, whose position appears from the following report :—

13th September 1720. George Graves haveing a Brother who receives the Dues for the Duke of Rutland of most of the

* " It obtained the name of Witherite, from its having been discovered by Dr. Withering, who first noticed it at Anglesark in Lancashire, in a vein, with sulphuret of lead, and some ores of zinc. . . . etc." Phillips. Mineralogy. 1816.

Mines of Derbyshire there, and who knows the most valuable Works there and the Customs and Manner of taking the Ground, has given him Orders to take at Three severl Places 100 Meres at each Place at the Forefields of good old Works and enter them in the Barr-Masters books which gives a sufficient Title and will cost but 12d. per meer entering. Now he proposes this shall be done for ye Company on the following terms vizt.—

The Company to pay 12d. per meer for as many meers as shall be taken up and no other Obligation or Charge, Unless they are approved by their Agent and on his Approbation to give the said George Graves and his Brother 50 Guineas for which said sum they will do all further service in the Country they can ; But in case Thomas Graves shall be found and thought fit to act as an agent for the Company to have a Reasonable Salary for the Same ; This Thomas Graves lives at Bakewell, is a Receiver of all the tenths as was his Father before him, abt. 32 years of age, hath a great Aquaintance and well beloved in the Country and well aquainted with the affairs thereof to whom Thomas Barker may be Recommended.

In this report we see several fragments of the ancient laws and customs of lead mining, particularly in the office of Barr Master, and lease of mine veins by the Mere, a measure varying from about 27 yards to 33 yards, and originally defined as the distance along the vein to which a miner, standing in the vein to the depth of his waist, could throw a " hack " or pick.

This report was followed by the taking of several leases in the parishes of Winster and Wensley, near Matlock. Most of the veins proved productive, and the Company found it necessary to have their own smelt mill on the spot, so purchased the lease of Bowers Mill, Ashover, and renewed it from time to time until 1778. The old furnaces were taken out and the reverberatory furnace both for smelting and refining put in their place. This became one of the most efficient mills in Derbyshire, and after a while most other mills in the area adopted the reverberatory or " cupola " furnace, so that in 1811 Farey, writing on the minerals of Derbyshire could say that :—

The Cupolas or low arched Reverberatory furnaces now exclusively used for the Smelting of Lead Ore in Derbyshire, were introduced from Wales by a company of Quakers . . .

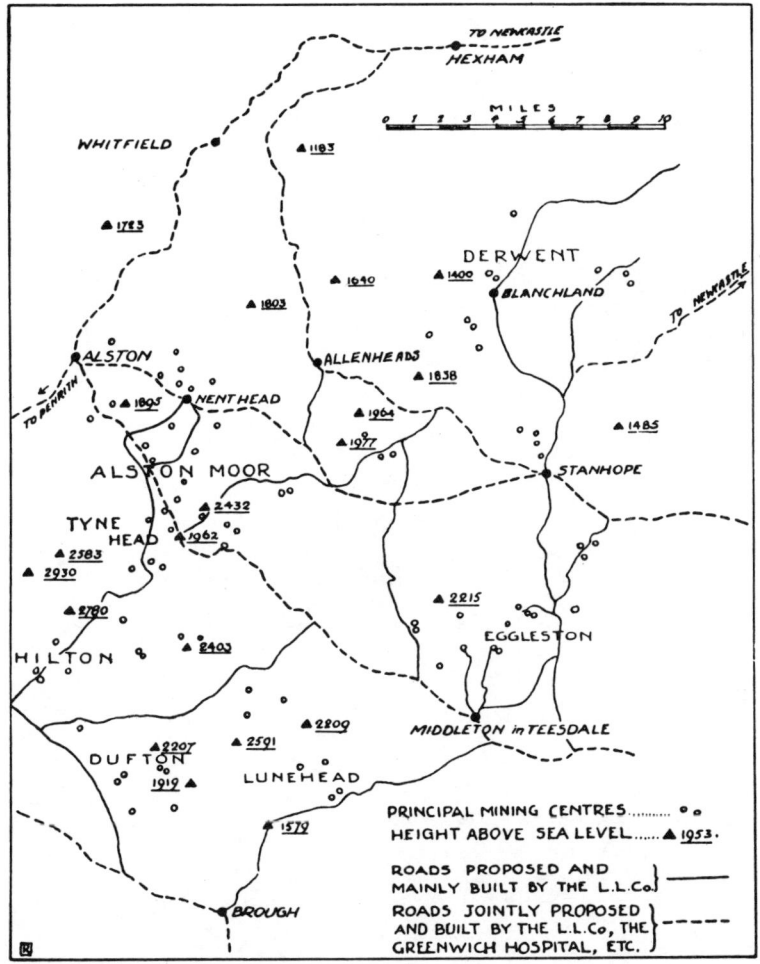

Map 3 Roads built by the London Lead Company in the North of England.

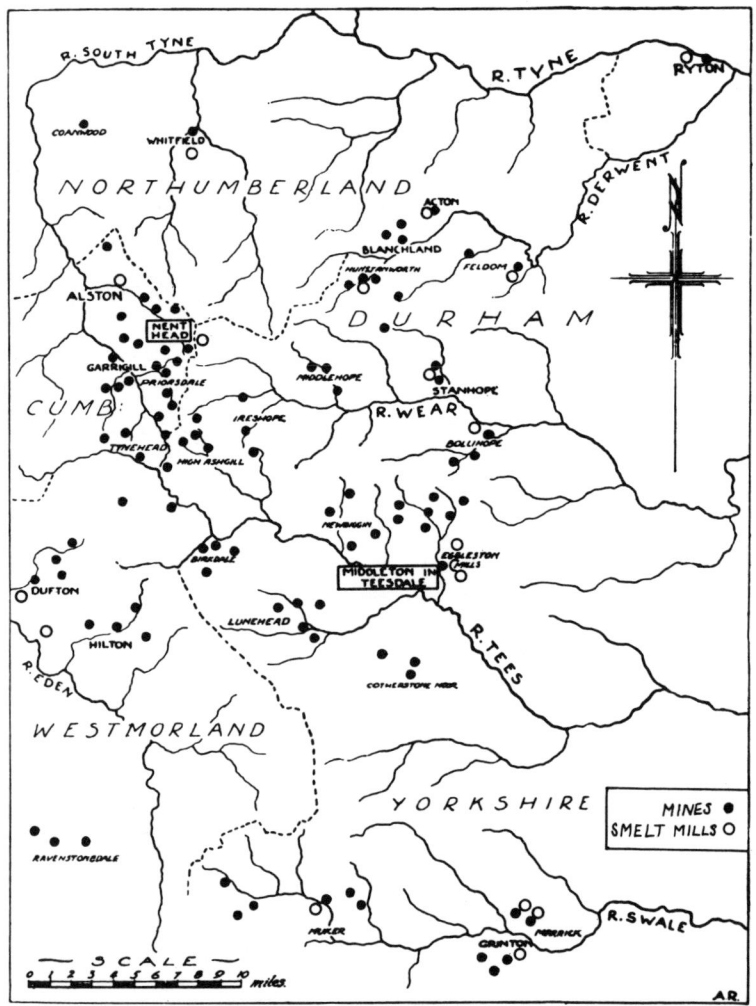

Map 4 The principal mine leases of the London Lead Company in the North of England.

There is no indication in the minutes that the suggestion of the appointment of Thomas Graves as agent for Derbyshire was accepted. Reports of processes and production continue to be received by the Court from Barker, the agent at Gadlis, until the appointment of Joseph Whitfield as resident agent at Bowers Mill in 1735. Joseph Whitfield was sent from Allendale in the northern area, and remained in charge of the Derbyshire ventures until 1778, when he returned to Allendale. The Derbyshire undertaking was remarkably self-contained and of considerable importance. The centre of their activity was the now famous Mill Close Mine where they made historic experiments with the steam engine and with deep level drainage (see a fuller account of the Derbyshire works, Raistrick, " Mill Close Mine ", *Proc. Durham University Phil. Soc.*, 1937). The famous Yatestoop Sough and Cowley Sough (Sough is the local name for a deep drainage tunnel) were driven by them during this period. As we have seen, Whitfield took active part in the promotion of both road and canal schemes which led to the greater development of the Derbyshire mining field.

In 1780 the Welsh agent added to the ore being smelted at Gadlis considerable quantities from the Isle of Man, and in 1782 the Company leased and developed the Great Laxey Mine, later sold by them to the Duke of Atholl for £1,250. In the latter part of the eighteenth century the numerous Welsh mines of the Company were being pushed more and more below ground water level, so that in the '80's practically everywhere they were faced with rapidly increasing water pumping costs. Between 1781 and 1789 a loss of £9,099 was incurred and on the recommendation of the Court the mill and stock at Gadlis were sold for £700 and the mine leases surrendered. At the same time the ventures in Derbyshire and the Isle of Man were sold and all efforts concentrated in the North of England.[9]

The Company's interest in lead mines at Wanlock Head between 1709 and 1730 has already been mentioned in connection with the Friendly Mining Society. While in Edinburgh contact was made with the Earl of Morton, who owned the mineral rights of the Orkney Islands. In 1710 Wright and Hall reported this to the Governor and Court, and instructions were sent to Allsopp to take William Gibson from London and some miners from Newcastle to examine the various mining sites in the Orkneys, sending samples for assay to London. The results of this venture, to which reference has already been made, were not very impressive. The Company's men explored a number of veins and opened out a few shafts and adits, but never produced ore on a commercial scale. The mines were only tested by the London Lead Company, and the scheme was soon allowed to lapse, but the places opened by them were worked intermittently through the eighteenth and early nineteenth centuries by individuals and by small associations.

The search in Scotland was by no means satisfied when Wanlock and Orkney had been tried. Various smaller localities were visited, but no serious work was undertaken until 1721, when the Alva silver mine, Stirling, came within their reach.[10] When the full story of this mine can be written up, it will provide a romance equal in interest to many of the mines in the New World.

Alva Mine, " in the Parish of Alva, five miles from Stirling East and by North ", belonged to Sir John Erskine about 1712 but was forfeited by him when he joined the Pretender in the rebellion of 1715. As Master of the Mint, Sir Isaac Newton took charge of the investigation of the silver yield of the mine and its valuation for the Crown, and commissioned Dr. Justus Brandshagen and James and Thomas Hamilton to report on the mine and to " smelt the ore buried in casks by Sir John Erskine's house ". This is a reference to a rather earlier report :—

From these two veins Sir John Erskine had the ore out of which he received 134 ounces of fine silver. . . . And after Sir John went to the rebels, Mr. Hamilton by the order of the Lady Erskine, had the oversight and direction of four miners who dug the ore from those two veins about four months together or something above, and put it up in old casks (hogsheads and barrels, etc.) to the quantity of about 40 tunns of ore, more or less, and hid the casks on the north-west side of the house, just by the gate of the house.

Brandshagen reported this to be some of the best silver ore he had seen in any part of Europe. The London Lead Company's minutes of 1721 say that :—

The mine was wrought a little by him (Sir J.E.) but forfeited on his joining the Pretender. Several trials have been made and reported by the Lords of the Treasury and Officers of the Mint. Sir John has got his pardon at the request of the Czar (of Russia) who was a near relation—so the mine is restored to him.

Details of the mine follow, and of the conclusion of the lease, with partition of shares, provision for royalties, etc. As some indication of the complexity of many of these early leases, the Alva mine was held for mining in thirteenths, the Company taking eleven-thirteenths and Erskine two-thirteenths; and for smelting in twentieths, the Company eleven-twentieths, Erskine seven-twentieths and the Crown one-tenth. The joint lease was operated for ten years but finally surrendered in 1731, when overhead charges were rapidly increasing.

In addition to these numerous ventures in Scotland, the Company from its northern centre examined and took leases of mines in Wensleydale and Swaledale, Yorks. These consisted of three separate groups; the reversion of the lease of mines in Grinton, with a smelt mill, was purchased for £2,625. In 1747 mines, manor and smelt mill of Marrick were leased for 31 years. In 1734 the Company leased from Edward Wortley Montague all the mines in upper Wensleydale in the manor and forest granted to the Earl of Lennox at the dissolution of Jervaulx Abbey, i.e. for practical purposes the mines in Sargill, Cotterdale and Lunds. At the same time the Company negotiated for the mineral leases in the former estates of Phillip Lord Wharton, which at the confiscation of his estates in 1729 on charge of high treason had been reserved to his sister, and by marriage passed later to the Earl of Pontefract. In the following years other small leases were added from time to time, until by 1747 a fairly widespread series of mines was held by the Company throughout Swaledale and Wensleydale, with one small mine in Wharfedale.

Throughout this early period the mining advisers as well as financiers of the Company had been the original Royal Mines members, Edward Wright, John Haddon, Urban Hall and Samuel Davies. They had travelled round all the mines, designed works, reported on markets, processes, legal points etc., and had in fact been the Company. Dr. Wright retired in 1727 and died the following year, and the others were becoming old men, so that the widely-spread new ventures lacked the oversight and personal contacts that alone could have justified them. This, taken along with the state of the lead market, caused the affairs of the Company to become somewhat difficult, and several expedients had to be adopted to obtain liquid capital. It seemed doubtful at certain stages whether the Company should develop purely as smelters and refiners of bought ore, or should become a large mining corporation; in all this uncertainty, however, the Company stuck close to the sale of silver to the Mint, and to the improvement of silver extraction methods. With the passing of this group of original members, an almost entirely strange personnel was elected to the Court of Assistants, and before long, starting in 1730, a quiet revolution in the affairs of the Company took place. It was under this new directorate that the rather poor properties of the Yorkshire leases were taken on.

Until 1881 the Company plodded steadily on, spending a good proportion of its income on improving mining and smelting, in cutting deep adits for exploration and drainage, and in developing the property on its leases. Headquarters were built at Middleton-in-Teesdale, schools, houses, roads, etc., built in that district as well as in Alston Moor. The Company managed to maintain a steady dividend, but towards the end of the period began to feel the general decline in lead markets that had set in all over the country, and so looked for possible reduction of their undertaking. With the sale of Alston Moor in 1882 went most of the leases in Weardale, and in 1883 the Company was left with no interest outside Teesdale. The old form of Governor and Company with a charter of incorporation and a weekly Court meeting, being rather clumsy for the continuance of the business, the whole concern was made into a limited liability company by decision of the Court, December 1883. Steady but small profits were being made, and their smelting technique still improved, so that frequent minutes note the preference of the markets for London Lead Company lead so long as it is available.

The decision to reduce the capital of the Company was taken at a Court meeting, July 16th, 1895, in a minute under several headings :—

THE LATER YEARS OF THE COMPANY, 1882-1905

1. That the Capital of the Company be reduced to £76,000 by writing off £19,000, part of the loss shown on the Balance Sheet.

2. That the sum of £294.9.10, part of the ascertained profit of the last half year, be applied to writing off the balance of loss then standing to Debit of the Profit and Loss.

3. That the estimated value of the Mining Leases be written down from £20,000 to £15,000.

4. That the amount of £5,000 now standing to Suspense account (provision for unclaimed shares and dividends) be written off.

5. That the Balance of Profit, £2,464.10.5, for the last half year, be placed to a separate account as suggested in the Directors' report to the Proprietors.

Many further minutes were considered and passed on forms of notice, and purely technical business points.

There was no question of the Company losing money, but the whole closure, or rather restriction of activity, seemed to spring from two sources : first a rapidly shrinking market characteristic of all lead mining in this country at the same period, and secondly the main members of the Court were getting old and tired and it was becoming very difficult to continue the Court government within the structure of the new limited liability company. An infusion of young blood might have tided over the difficulties, but judging by the experience of all other mining concerns, the Governor and Court of Assistants were remarkably foresighted and wise in their decisions. The Duke of Devonshire's great lead mining undertakings in the Grassington district of Yorkshire finally closed down in 1896, and have never been reopened. The great Beaumont group in the North were considerably reduced in 1865, and finally shut down except one or two small ventures about 1890, and a similar story could be told in almost all areas. The accounts show definite profits during all the time of the discussions just mentioned, and the profits continued to the end.

Profit half year ending	15th May, 1897	£7,024	14	1
,, ,, ,, ,,	30th Oct., ,,	6,563	6	2
,, ,, ,, ,,	14th May, 1898	4,642	15	7
,, ,, ,, ,,	31st Oct., ,,	2,809	1	10
,, ,, ,, ,,	13th May, 1899	2,020	4	7

The steady decrease in these figures keep pace with the gradual decrease in the men employed and the closure of mines. This is perhaps best shown in the quarterly wages bills :—

		£			£
1894	Oct.	6,080	1898	Jan.	4,281
1895	Jan.	5,800		Apl.	4,160
	Apl.	4,340		Jul.	3,922
	Jul.	4,775		Oct.	3,580
	Oct.	4,721	1899	Jan.	3,570
1896	Jan.	4,628		Apl.	3,263
	Apl.	4,379		Jul.	2,796
	Jul.	4,434		Oct.	2,430
	Oct.	4,120			
1897	Jan.	4,675			
	Apl.	4,100			
	Jul.	4,081			
	Oct.	4,066			

As the final minute book, 1899-1905, has not yet been discovered, and as the last members of the Court are now passed away, the actual end of the Company must be left somewhat obscure. It is clear, however, from more than one source that the final winding up was completed about March 1905, when, unfortunately, many of the remaining papers of the Company were destroyed. When the story can be completed, there must be inevitably a feeling of sadness in probing the closing stages of a concern that had weathered all the vicissitudes of two centuries, passing through the whole of the Industrial Revolution, and spreading its net over England, Wales, Ireland, the Orkneys and the Isle of Man. Their name, however, still lives in traditions that have a very warm place in the hearts of the Alston Moor people, and the monument to the Company is seen in villages, schools, roads and plantations scattered over all the areas they worked and served.

NOTES TO CHAPTER V

[1] Other Chartered Companies for which petitions were received were: The Company of Mine Adventurers; The Governor and Company of Lead Miners in England and Wales; The Governor and Company for digging and working mines and for beating and refining

ore in England . . ., etc., etc. There is no evidence that any of these became active.

[2] Two works are mentioned, one "the Cupola works at Bristol" and the other the "cupola at the Bridge at Rownham". This latter was bought out by the company, to cut out competition. "The works att ye Cupola are fitt to be sett on worke immediately. There are 5 furnaces requiring four men to each. Wages 10/- a week, one with another, some more, some less. Can command 12 men if need be, who understand the working. Each furnace will melt 12 tun a week of oar, making 9 tun of lead from Welsh oar. "We believe some 20 tuns oar may be bought near works."

[3] A minute was passed on March 23rd, 1695, passing back the Bristol works to Clerk. "Sir Talbot Clerk to pay £86.15.6 for lead ore and iron at the works and to take possession of the Cupola, tools, etc. He and the others concerned in his 500 shares to enjoy it without claim from the subscribers of the other 500 shares.

"If they act under the present charter, to pay Thomas Renda for the use of the other 500 shareholders, half the cost of obtaining the charter, vizt, £120.19.8", etc.

[4] Grandison's patent was granted in 1678 for smelting lead in the reverberatory furnace, using pit coal, and was one of many such patents attempted at that time, though most of them proved unsuccessful. The existence of this patent blocked the way for other people to try similar smelting methods. The patent expired in 1692, so that Vernatti and Addison lost no time in applying for the charter of the Governor and Company, with which we are concerned, which would allow them to smelt lead with coal.

Thomas Addison, who is associated with Constantine Vernatti in the Charter, and was Deputy Governor of the Company, was the leading man in another rather similar concern, "The Governor and Company for making iron with pit coal". This Company was formed to work an invention patented by Addison in 1692 and got its charter in 1693 with Sir John Lowther as first Governor, and several of the men of the Lead Company also, as Talbot Clerk, George Moor, and Thomas Renda. Vernatty and Barkstead were members of the Company of Copper Miners of England.

[5] The fuller story of the German Miners at Keswick is told by W. G. Collingwood, in "Elizabeth Keswick", Cumberland and Westmorland Antiquarian and Archæological Society Tract, Series VIII, 1912. The Company, or Society of Royal Mines, was founded towards the end of 1564. After preliminary negotiations for two years, in 1564, December 10th, an Indenture was made between Queen Elizabeth on the one part, and Thomas Thurland and Daniel Hechstetter on the other part, by which these two were empowered to "search, dig, try, roast, and melt, all manner of mines and ures of gold, silver, copper and quicksilver, in the counties of York, Lancaster, Cumberland, Westmorland, Cornwall, Devon, Gloucester, and Worcester, and in Wales".

Daniel Hechstetter was acting as the agent for David Haug, Hans Langnauer & Company, of Augsburg, Germany, linen drapers and silk merchants. They had branches in most of the important towns of Europe from Vienna to Antwerp, and from Cracow to Lyons, and though not originally interested in mining, they had recently taken over from the successors of the famous house of the Fuggers, the control of the copper mines of Neusohl in Northern Hungary. One of their branches was at Schwatz in the Tyrol, near Innsbruck, and from that centre the first batch of miners was sent over to Keswick to open out the copper mines of that district. After flourishing for a period under the charter of Elizabeth, the mines in Cumberland and a smaller group in Cornwall came upon hard times, and the concern was largely carried on at a loss by a group of German and London business men. Hechstetter, the first manager, died in 1581, and among his successors, Ulrich Frass was sent to Neath in South Wales in 1586, where he introduced improved methods of copper smelting. This branch of the Company eventually came under the influence of Sir Humphrey Mackworth in the latter half of the seventeenth century. The smelting works and mines at Keswick were destroyed in 1651 during the Civil Wars and little is known of their work between about 1580 and that event. In 1600 the Germans had started works in the Coniston district, which they abandoned in 1650, but these were re-opened in 1690, along with some of the smaller mines near Caldbeck, Cumberland, and some in Wales, and in 1692 we find Dr. Wright concerned in all these as Chairman of the Society of Royal Mines Copper. This was evidently the descendant and successor of the original chartered Company of the Germans, and became the parent company of the Quaker Lead Company now under consideration. How the succession was obtained by Wright is a complete mystery, and must be the subject of research in the future.

[6] The original share capital of the London Lead Company was in 1692, 1,000 shares of £18 each. No person was to be eligible for nomination to the Court of Assistants unless he held not less than 10 shares.

[7] Silver returns are traceable through the minute books in the following form, e.g. :—

10th July, 1705. Treasurer reports a note received for the delivery of six cakes of silver, 290 ozs. 15 dwts.

17th July, 1705. One cake of silver from North, 79 oz. 10 dwts.

Treasurer has received silver from the North 51 lbs. 5 ozs. 10 dwts. and delivered this to the Mint. By assay this was 14 dwts. better (than standard purity) and in standard are 54 lbs. 8 ozs. 8 dwts. at 5/4d per ounce is £169.11.6 . . .

The Treasurer returns from the Mint,

    Ingot No. 2   44 lbs. 11 ozs. 5 dwts. fine.
    that is   47 ,, 10 ,, 9 ,, standard.
    at 5/2 per ounce is £148.8.0.

NOTES TO CHAPTER V

[8] The following data is attached to the minutes proposing and agreeing to the closure of the Welsh Mines.

Alston Moor Mines.

The Company have gained by :— in 9 years

	£	s.	d.
Scaleburn Moss	2051	12	3
Small Cleugh	794	11	7
Browngill Sun Vein	3250	12	0
Mannorgill	6055	0	5
East Flakebrigg	865	11	4
Green Mines	180	14	4
Rampgill	492	8	3
Middle Cleugh	1524	3	0
Shawfoot	129	7	0
	15343	11	0

have lost by :— in 9 years

	£	s.	d.
Gudamgill Mines Moss	291	10	3
Browngill	1335	15	3
Wiregill	343	1	5
Holmhead	542	12	7
Shildon	2333	1	8
Jeffrys	211	15	5
Whitfield mine	979	9	8
	6037	6	3

therefor the gain is £9306 4 9
Profit in Wales in 9 years is £3748 18 4
which is rather more than 4% on Capital employed.

Mines are wrought by farm but produced only 63 tons last year. Co. must therefor look to smelting bought lead, from which little prospect of gain. Undertaking presents so unpromising an aspect that they hope Co. will consider whether to continue.

Profit and Loss on Gadlis including Isle of Man.

	Loss				Gain		
1781	890	5	7	1783	771	1	0
1782	1665	16	1	1784	448	17	4
1786	160	18	3	1785	414	13	6
1787	4389	4	7	1788	755	17	3
1789	783	9	11				
Interest of Capl.							
9 yrs. @ 4%	3600	0	0	Balance is Loss	9099	5	4
	11489	14	5		11489	14	5

[9] Report by agents, 16.9.1805 :—
1 Axletree of wheel at Eggleston Mill broken and a new wheel necessary but old one might mend for this season.

Eggleston Mill will smelt in present state 400 bing per month
Nent Head ,, ,, ,, ,, ,, ,, 270 ,, ,, ,,
Acton ,, ,, ,, ,, ,, ,, 327 ,, ,, ,,
Whitfield ,, ,, ,, ,, ,, ,, 300 ,, ,, ,,
─────
1297

Messrs. Skottow & Lord Crewes Trustees are about to grant a lease of mineral ground and Acton Mill to Easterby Hall and Co. at expiry of our lease which is 1¾ years.

Stanhope Mill is equally well situated and has 2 blast furnaces a reducing hearth and refinery and room for enlargement or new building for an air furnace which would enable it to smelt 327 bings per month and a horizontal chimney may be erected. All mills now in full work and 12000 pces lead will be made from 1st Aug. to end of the year, 6000 of which will be got down to the wharfe.

It is clear from the above that Stanhope Mill was being redesigned to take the place exactly of Acton which they were soon to surrender.

Their lead was carried from Acton, Whitfield, and Nent Head, to the original wharf on the river Tyne at Stella, near Blaydon. This had been leased in 1706 and remained in use as their shipping wharf until 1836, when railway carriage from Alston became generally used. Bourn's *History of Ryton* says, " The road by which the lead was conveyed to the wharf was called *Lead Gate*. The route was from the mines, over Hedley Fell to Lead Gate, where the ponies were changed ; they then proceeded by the road past Coalburns, Greenside, and Path Head to Stella. . . . Every ton of ore produced nine or ten ounces of silver and from this fact, the road from Blaydon Church to Winlaton was called *Silver Hill*."

[10] The selection of such apparently distinct areas as Wanlock Head and Stirling, by the Lead Company, was perhaps not so casual as it seems, when we consider the existence of the so-called Scots Mining Company. This had been founded by Sir John Erskine of Alva, Stirling, and financed by the Sun Fire Office, of London. Soon after 1715 the Scots Mining Company leased Leadhills mines, adjoining Wanlock Head, and no doubt it was here that Wright and others became known to Erskine and received their information about the Alva Mine from him.

Brooke, G. C. discusses the Quaker coinage in " The Coinage with Roses and Plumes". *Numismatic Chronicle*, 5th series, XIV, 1934.

Hunt, C. J. *Lead Miners of the North Pennines in the eighteenth and nineteenth centuries.* Manchester University Press, 1970. This is a study of social and economic conditions and has much reference to the London Lead Company.

Raistrick, A. " Lead Smelting in the North Pennines during the 17th and 18th centuries." *Proc. Univ. Durham Philosophical Society.* 1936, 164-179.

Rees, W. *Industry before the Industrial Revolution.* Cardiff 1968, vol 2, 504-21, The London Lead Company.

CHAPTER VI

Technical Developments—Smelting—Drainage—Ore dressing—Ventilation

THE account so far given of the London Lead Company has been focussed mainly upon the social work and the organisation of the Company and the technical processes of mining and smelting have had only incidental mention. Yet in any balanced view of the history it soon becomes evident that the relationship between the social, economic and technical aspects is one of very intimate inter-dependence. Chapter V opens with a suggestion that " the social policy was the product mainly of three factors "—and then lists them as (*a*) the natural isolation of the Company's working areas, remoteness from markets, etc; (*b*) experience of the value of healthy and contented workpeople; (*c*) the strong Quaker element among the Court and officials of the Company. It is further stated that " willingness to experiment and insistence on technical progress is characteristic of many of the early Quaker industrialists, and no doubt was a main factor in leading to the expansion and success of their enterprises, which made their extended social work possible."

We started the book with an account of the building of Nent Head village, followed by the provision of many social amenities, some of them well in advance of the general practice of the time. The village was made necessary to house the number of employees brought together by the location of a new smelt mill and dressing floors in a position central to many of the Company's mines. The site of the smelt mill, near the head of the Nent Valley, and to which the village was related, was dictated by the occurrence and disposition of the Rampgill Vein and its rich associated complex of veins and not by any choice such as an independent planner might have made. With such a creation of a new community many miles from the small town of Alston, the need for providing services arose and if these were provided on a scale more generous than was often the case, this generosity rested only in part on the particular Quaker outlook of the Company and in part on the economic value of a stable and contented group of employees, housed near to their work.

Many of the provisions made by the Company for the well-being of its workpeople and detailed in the earlier chapters, could be credited to excellent business instinct and might be claimed as philanthropy or paternalism which paid a profit. We do not accept this as a total view but prefer to look to the compulsions of technical advances and of what now-a-days might be called rationalisation within the Company's undertakings as contributing factors. In this view the building of Nent Head and the comparable centre at Masterman Place at Middleton in Teesdale rank equally with and are linked to, advances in smelting methods, mine organisation and other technical aspects of the industry.

In attempting some evaluation of the technical progress of the Company it will be found convenient to relate the discussion to three phases of its history. The first phase lasted from 1697 to 1730 or thereabouts; a second phase followed to 1810 and a third to 1880. These dates are by no means rigid but are useful generalisations to keep in mind. They leave out the earliest years of the Charter and the last twenty-five years when the Company was first contracting and then closing down its interests.

The dominant figure of the first phase was Dr. Edward Wright and it is to him that we owe the development of the reverberatory furnace. The most significant event was the design and building of the Gadlis Smelt Mill in 1703-4 at Bagilt near Flint, North Wales. Here the reverberatory furnaces were at work and Wright and Anthony Barker, his manager, applied them to lead smelting and refining and to the recovery and refining of silver. Many problems arose in this work. Wright was concerned in the Ryton Company, and with the absorption of this into the Governor and Company the " Quaker Company " emerged. The silver-rich lead ores which were smelted at Ryton helped to establish the new company as a prime supplier of pure silver

Plate XII   Mine " shop " and tips at Smallcleugh Level, Nent Head.

Plate XIII   Old mine tips planted by the London Lead Company, with later tips unplanted.

Plate XIV Gadlis Lead Smelting Mill at Bagillt, Flintshire, about 1720. (Drawn by Miss L. M. Simcock from William Williams's map of Flintshire and Denbighshire. *Clwyd Record Office*)

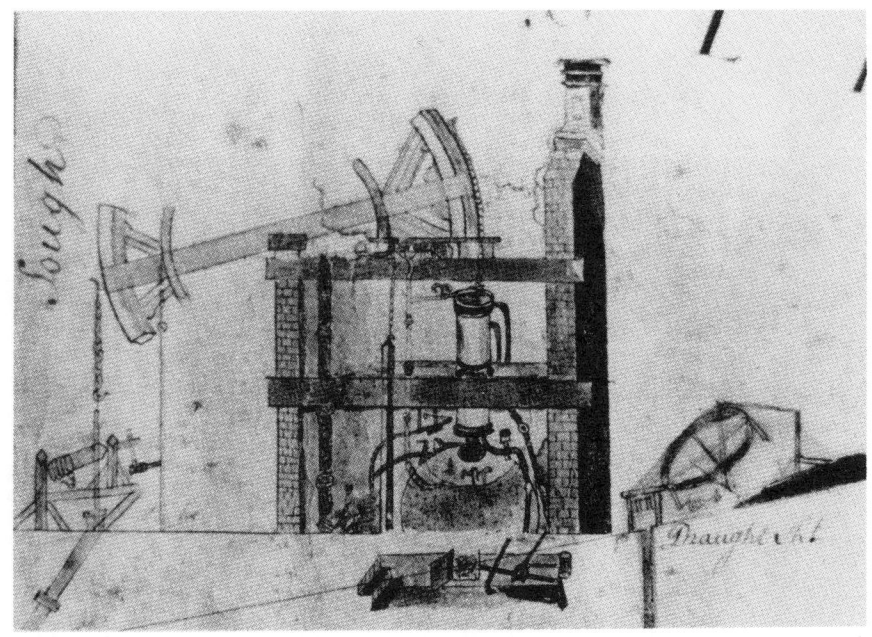

Plate XV The Newcomen steam pumping-engine built at the London Lead Company's Mill Close Mine at Winster, Derbyshire in 1748.

to the Mint (Chapter V). For the silver recovery large quantities of bone ashes were used and many improvements in their preparation and use were made at Gadlis where silver refining also was carried out. With an increasing demand for silver, the Company were tempted to follow up many reports of mines and soon had leases as far scattered as the south of Ireland, the Pennines, Central Scotland and the Orkneys. None of these were large mineral fields but all were isolated mines of no great size and with slender reserves, and for an adequate supply of lead they had to turn to the North Wales ores which had a comparatively low silver content. Research led them to the production of what was called a " merchantable " (soft) lead, from a variety of ores, and the increasing demand for lead directed attention to acquiring more lead mines rather than silver mines. The difficulties of transport and remote management soon brought some of the far scattered mines to closure and by 1740 they were concentrating their work on large groups of mines in Wales, Derbyshire and the north Pennines.

Gadlis was a large mill with many buildings, almost a small hamlet in itself, and closely associated with houses for the manager and some staff; many of the craftsmen and officials were engaged at a salary with house and coals provided.[1] Gadlis was not far from the mines which the Company leased and worked, and the benefits arising from a compact community and from the close and easy contact between mines and smelt mill were soon apparent. Barker's management brought mines and smelt mill into an integrated group in Wales and showed up the inefficiencies and disadvantage of being only a smelting group dependent upon rather precarious and very remote sources of ore. Alongside the Welsh development, ores purchased in Derbyshire were tried out at Gadlis and when found to be good, leases of Derbyshire mines were taken around the villages of Wensley and Winster. The Gadlis pattern was followed in the lease of Bower's Mill, a smelt mill fairly centrally placed among the new mine leases, and in the appointment of Joseph Whitfield a little later, as general manager of both mining and smelting in Derbyshire.

Bower's mill was already equipped with ore-hearths which served for several years during which the mining leases were being extended and a more urgent problem of unwatering some of the old mines and providing adequate drainage for the new ones was being tackled. The Derbyshire mining field is traditionally (and in practice) the home of the " sough " or drainage tunnel, driven from a low point on some stream side, and going under the mineral ground to be worked, thus becoming a permanent drain for the developing mines. Almost the first work of the Company was the driving of a " sough " and later by their driving of a sough and use of a steam engine for pumping at their famous Mill Close Mine, they made an important contribution to mining practice.[2]

Throughout the North Pennine areas worked by the Company, the topography was such that most of their mines could be reached by adits and the planning, driving and linking up of complex systems of adits, and the scarcity of shafts became a characteristic feature of their development work.

At Bower's Mill some experience of ore-hearth smelting was gained but an early change over to reverberatory furnaces was planned and carried out. The reverberatory furnace had become so much the key to their successful search for high quality lead that the construction of their later furnaces was a closely guarded secret. Masons like Joseph Dickenson of Nettle Hill, Allendale, were employed under a bond of £100 to build reverberatory furnaces for the Company under instruction, but were bound not to build any similar furnace for anyone else for twenty years on pain of forfeiting the bond. Dickenson and some others were employed at Nent Head and also were sent to Derbyshire to help at the reconstruction of Bower's Mill.

In Alston Moor a new era began in the mining field when the government, and then the Greenwich Hospital, took over the forfeited estates of Lord Derwentwater (see Introduction). The Lead Company had a number of widely scattered mine leases dating from the early days of the Ryton Company, with smelt mills at Blagill, Whitfield and

Ryton. When the government confiscated the estates, Colonel George Liddell secured a lease of ground at the head of the Nent Valley and floated a company which from 1738 to 1745 began to develop the rich Rampgill Vein very near to the present Nent Head. This vein had been discovered about 1690 but only worked on a very small scale. Near the mine Liddell built a smelt mill in which he designed, according to his prospectus, to have no less than nine furnaces. His grandiose schemes failed and in 1745 the London Lead Company purchased the transfer of his leases and the mill. They redesigned the mill with improved ore hearths, and taking the lesson of Gadlis to heart, housed their smelters near the mill and in August 1746 began smelting there the very considerable output of ore from the Rampgill complex. The addition of many more leases around Nent Head soon created a very compact field with a central mill and new dressing floors placed near the Rampgill Mine entrance. Thus began Nent Head.[3]

In the years following the completion of the mill the Company were able to change from leasing individual mines to the practice of leasing large areas or estates within which many veins occurred. Larger dressing floors central to the new and larger leases were made, but the ore from individual mines or even from single veins, was kept separate, assayed and either smelted separately or on occasion was used to select a mixture of ores to make a lead of a particular quality.

The mill and floors at Nent Head were for some years fully occupied in dealing with output from the Rampgill and adjacent leases, and Whitfield and Acton (Derwent) Mills dealt with the rest. At Acton much of the lead from other mills was refined for silver. The improved reverberatory furnaces which had been put into Whitfield Mill needed, in order to work at the maximum efficiency, a finely ground and properly graded ore. Thus stamps were being made and used at the Derwent mines in 1737, much earlier than the date which Pryce ascribes to them for their introduction in Cornwall. In the mines in the Derwent field air pipes were introduced for forced underground ventilation and gunpowder was used in driving in hard ground. Waterwheels were built along with pumps from below the drainage level.

The advances in this area of Nent Head and Derwent can be indicated by the fact that during this period the output of refined silver increased from 6,673 ounces in 1738 to 15,647 ounces in 1765, and when Nent Head mill was fully establishd the production increased still further; by 1825 when a new process for the separation of silver (Pattinson's) was introduced, the annual output of silver had exceeded 26,000 ounces and the production of lead was between 5,000 and 6,000 tons per annum.

Teesdale leases were taken in 1753 and an old mill at Egglestone was eventually replaced by three mills with reverberatory furnaces which served the whole of Teesdale and its tributaries. These mills soon became the scene of experimental work. In 1787 there is an entry in the Court minutes of the trial of an air furnace (reverberatory) against a blast hearth (ore-hearth) which proved the reverberatory to have a great advantage over the ore-hearth, so the Court ordered that reverberatories were to be used in all their mills.[4]

By 1790 both the Derbyshire and Welsh concerns had been sold, along with others in Yorkshire and those on the Derwent, so that the whole activity of the Company was now concentrated in Alston Moor, Weardale and Teesdale. Nent Head village was enlarged and the Middleton in Teesdale estate was build in response to the increase in activity in all sections of the Company's work. The modernised transport plan with new roads and many improved older ones, and the participation in turnpike roads which had marked the last two decades of the eighteenth century was brought to completion in the opening years of the nineteenth and proved to be of the greatest value in drawing the northern area into a single manageable form.

The story of the social welfare provisions—housing, medical, educational and recreational—which followed in the nineteenth century has been told in the earlier chapters, but the technical progress was not described. Although it cannot be dealt with here in detail, still some mention should be made of it. In 1823 Edward Hawke Locker and

John Taylor (the Cornish mining engineer) in their report to the Commissioners for the Greenwich Hospital on the state of their Alston Moor Mines say

> Most of the important improvements in Mining have been introduced by them [the London Lead Company]. Their levels at Nent Head extend nearly twenty miles underground and are still carrying on with great spirit . . . after the War the London Lead Company steadily continued to work their mines at a heavy loss and but for this the Parish of Aldstone must have been involved in one common ruin.

They note that the Company are spending £6,000 a year on trials and keep complete plans of all their workings. Taylor adds a further note that they are using rail road levels instead of shafts and that they are doing much experimental work with reverberatory furnaces in Teesdale (at the Egglestone Mills).

If we could have visited the moor, say about 1820, we would have seen abundant differences from the area as it was towards the end of the eighteenth century. More mines were at work but the ore they produced was carried to fewer dressing floors. Instead of a crowd of boys and women breaking and crushing ore by hand, nearly all the floors now had crushing rollers powered by waterwheel. The use of rollers for crushing had been introduced by John Taylor at Wheal Crowndale near Tavistock in 1804 and were soon taken up by the London Lead Company in Alston Moor. They made modifications and improvements and in 1813 built three of their new-pattern crushers with three pairs of rollers and a two-stage action, at Lodgesyke in Teesdale, and at Rampgill and Smallcleugh at Nent Head.

Any lumpy material which escaped the rollers was treated in a set of stamps. The ground-up bouse was then treated in a series of buddles, but before 1820 most of the buddles had been replaced by mechanically driven hotching tubs, keives etc. The agent was able to report to the Court about the dressing floors at Dufton: " Here also we found proof of the superiority of our washing in being able to employ with profit a number of boys to re-wash old wastes that have been accumulated in 40 years." By 1827 further improvements in the design of the buddle were reported. The first stage in these improvements was based upon a new form of the buddle which was the basic apparatus of the processes for separating ore and rock in a stream of running water. The many forms of buddle were all of them only modifications of a long wooden trough with a flow of water down it, in which the mixed ore and rock in fine particles, was stirred about so that the rock was carried off and the ore left behind. In 1817 Stagg at Nent Head had made a model of a new and different kind of buddle and had some built for experiment. Over the years he modified them, moving the ore with mechanical paddles, changing the shape and eventually arriving at the circular buddle. At Nent Head the new buddle was tried out with slimes, the finest residues of the washings, and he reported that " when the attempt was first made to wash slime ores by this machine, it cost 42s. per bing; the present cost is 7s. per bing." The 1827 report says " the waste that used to be thrown out as valueless is now washed on the large mechanical buddles at a cost of 4s. 3d. per bing. The Company is the sole introducer of this improvement."

At Grassington Moor Captain Barrett had mechanised the hotching tub in which ore was separated by being shaken in a seive submerged in water and an early improvement of this was made by Petherick between 1828 and 1830. The Company were very quick to appreciate the value of inventions both by their own staff and by others and were generous in paying for the right to use them. By bringing together their own inventions and securing the use of others they had so far improved their dressing methods that they planned a redesign of all their dressing floors.

At the same time (1828) as the improved buddles were being installed on all the Company's floors, Stagg made the first " table " separator. It consisted of a flat table about 14ft 6in long and half that width with three raised sides so that it formed a shallow trough. It was hung up by chains at the four corners so arranged that the " table " had a tilt which could be varied. The table was so connected by levers and cams to a source of power, that it could be continuously shaken. Bouse (mixed ore and stone) ran over the table surface in a stream of water, and when the slope and the frequency and degree of shaking were properly adjusted a good separation of ore was obtained. This in improved forms still holds its position as an important part of any ore-dressing plant. In the neighbouring Allendale mines in 1847 an employee, Brunton, made a radical advance and patented a continuous cloth separator in which the rigid table was replaced by a continuous belt of cloth travelling round two rollers, the tight side at the top. This side was stiffened with wooden slats and tilted like the table. Slimes were fed onto it in a stream of water travelling in opposite direction to the movement of the cloth. The cloth dipped into a trough where the ore was washed off. The cost of labour was reduced by 50 per cent and the smelters said that a 5 per cent better concentrate was obtained. The London Lead Company at once approached the inventor and purchased the patent rights. Four of these were made and added to the Nent Head floors and four were installed in Teesdale. Only two years later a Company employee, Atwood, invented another machine for dealing with the most difficult of all material, the slimes. By an immediate application of all improvements their washing floors soon became some of the best in the country. The presence on them of an increasing amount of machinery forced upon the Company their next great advance. That was the move from open dressing floors, exposed to all the vagaries of weather, threatening the health of their dressers, to the enclosed " dressing mill " in which the machinery was not only protected as well as the workers, but it was soon possible to arrange it in a sequence which allowed a great measure of " flow " where the ore passed by gravity feed from one process to another.

As every process of dressing involved the use of water it is not strange that several hydraulic inventions were used. In the Teesdale mines a " water balance " was used at more than one place, in which the weight of water in a descending tub could hoist ore up a shaft. A more unusual and very efficient device was the " water blast." In this a stream of water was carried down a shaft in a pipe which had snore-hole inlets near the top by which the falling column of water drew in an amount of air with it. At the foot of the shaft the water fell into a closed tank or vessel in which the air was released and gathered above the outflow level of the water. This air was under pressure and could be forced through the workings for ventilation. At a later date in Nent Head an elaborated water blast was used at the Brewery Shaft to provide compressed air for the mines and was at work until recent years. Another machine made by the Company's engineers was a " water draught engine," to use their own name for it. This was a simple arrangement of two cylinders, one 28in diameter open upwards, and one 23in diameter, open downwards and working as a loose plunger inside the first. The air pipe to the mine had a rising branch up the middle of the outer cylinder, reaching to the level of the rim, and at the bottom had a clack or non-return valve to allow exit of air to the mine workings. The lower cylinder (the 28in one) was full of water to within a few inches of the top, and the inverted cylinder rim dipped

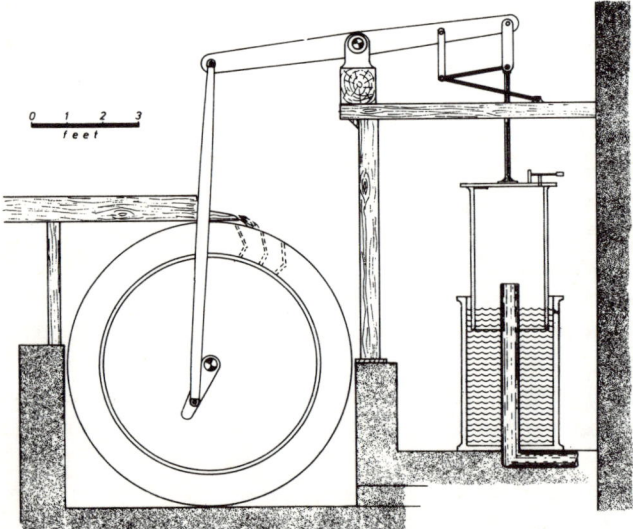

Fig 6 The air blowing machine developed by the London Lead Company for ventilating mines and blowing smelting-mill furnaces.

into this water, the air pipe thus entering the enclosed, water sealed space in the upper cylinder. This cylinder was attached through a parallel motion to the end of a rocking beam moved by a waterwheel. The top cylinder had two valves which opened during the up-stroke to admit air but closed on the down stroke so that the air was forced through the rising pipe into the mine. Several of these machines were built to a single pattern to run about 28 r.p.m. with 23in stroke to give 34.5 gallons of air a stroke, or nearly a thousand gallons of air per minute. Frequent minutes to the Court report on the wide use and reliability of this machine and its fairly wide adoption in smelt mills and in many neighbouring mines of other owners.[5]

With these many improvements the output of the Company's mines went up to exceed 12,000 tons of ore in the 1820s and then settled down to about 10,000 tons a year, as a normal figure in the mid-century. The extraction of silver which was about 35 to 40 thousand ounces up to 1835 rose to over 60,000 ounces per year when the new dressing mills and the general reconstruction came into work, but in the 1860s fell back to about 55,000 ounces.

It should be clear that the technical improvements and inventions cannot really be separated from the social conditions, organisation and training of the miners, but that each reacted upon the other and took an equal part in the story of this Company.

NOTES TO CHAPTER VI

[1] Minute Book of Royal Mines Copper, 3 Aug 1708 and Court Minute Book I, 13 March 1704.

[2] Raistrick A., " Mill Close Lead Mine." *Proc Univ Durham Phil Soc*, 1937, X, 38–47.

[3] Court Minute Book XI, Sept 1751.

[4] This order was not applied to all the mills, Nent Head mill continued to use ore hearths.

[5] These improvements are dealt with in more detail in Raistrick A. & Jennings B. *History of Lead Mining in the Pennines*, 1965, chaps 7 and 9.

CHAPTER VII

Biographical Notes on some Members of the Company.

IN the long history of the Quaker Lead Company, nothing is more disappointing than the very scant information that has been preserved about the personalities behind the concern, throughout its history. With the exception of a very few people, we still know nothing of the leaders and controllers of this Company in any part of its history. Friends' history and journals are alike silent about the industrial interests of many of the early Friends, and all the biographical material that can be found so far is limited to the occasional references in the minutes of the London Monthly Meetings for Friends between 1692 and 1710, so kindly provided for me by Irene L. Edwards, and the very scattered material for some of the people concerned with the Company between 1815 and 1865, for whom there are a few entries in the index to the letter books. Much of the information about Charles Alsopp has been contributed by John Hall Shield, a descendant of some of the early leaders in the Company.

It is probable that much material is still preserved among the family records of Friends, and perhaps in course of time some of this will be collected together to enable a fuller account of the pioneers of the Company to be written, which will make their work and achievements more understandable.

Dr. Edward Wright

So far as anything is clear from the early history of both the Ryton Company and the Royal Mines Copper Company of Wales, the parents of the Quaker Lead Company, Dr. Edward Wright stands out as the originator and prime mover of the whole concern.

London and Middlesex Quarterly Meeting Marriage Registers have the following entry:—

Edward Wright of Southwark Glass Grinder son of Nathaniel Wright of Guildford, Surrey, married Sarah Knight at Bull and Mouth 17.7.1685.

The Burial Registers give the following :—

SARAH WRIGHT died 19.9.1721 aged 78 of the Parish of St. Margarets New Fish Street, late wife of Doctor Edward Wright, buried Bunhill Fields.

Wright is referred to in the early minutes of the Company as " of the sign of the Shipp, near the Monument in London " and as Physician and Chemist. This will identify him with the Dr. Wright mentioned in a German work on mining (C. A. Schlüter, *Grundliche Unterricht von Huttenwerken*, etc., 1738), where the origin of the reverberatory furnace is being discussed, and Schlüter credits it to " three ingenious persons of whom one of the name of Wright, was a doctor of medicine and chemist, another a goldsmith, and the third an ingenious man who applied much time and money to it ". The other two would stand excellently for Freame and Haddon, or possibly for Matthews and Haddon, as Matthews is once mentioned as a goldsmith, and he certainly financed the earlier ventures of Wright. Smith and Houghton in their discussions of business both link together for remark the Quaker Glassgrinders and Lead Company, a further slight support for the marriage register Wright being our Wright. There is no record of his death to hand, beyond the statement made some time ago by Mr. Rhys Jenkins, that Wright the metallurgist and member of the Royal Mines Copper of Wales, had died in 1728 in Bath. That he did die in that year is confirmed from the minutes of the Company and the surrender of his shares.

In the minutes of the Meeting for Sufferings of the Society of Friends, Irene L. Edwards finds the following references to Wright and some other of the members of the London Lead Company :—

6.12.1707. Sussex. Rd Haylers case is continued to ye care of Thos Johnson and Edward Wright to assist him therein.

21.3.1708. Sussex. Edward Wright reports he has writ in Rd Haylers case as desired last meeting.

4.4.1708. Wales. John Field his and Nathanl Marks being with Colonel Bowles in the case of ye Welch Friend Imprest into his Regiment. That he told them he could not discharge him till he had recd a Certificate from the Justices that sent him into ye Regiment of his being a man of a Trade and that he rented

10 or 12 (? £) annum wch the Correspondents are continued to endeavour to procure.

And it being expected that the said friend will be obliged to march to Plymouth with the said Regiment Danl Phillips is desired to write to Henry Ceane on his behalf.

Also Edward Wright brot in a letter from Anthony Barker (he was the agent at Gadlis) intimating that he had spoken with one of the Justices (wch was agst ye sending said friend into ye Regiment) who promised to goe with him to ye other 3 to endeavour his discharge.

Edward Wright has ye letter.

11.4.1708. Gadlis. Anthony Barker to Edward Wright. That according to wt he writ in his last, did goe with Lloyd of Pontoholrin ? to . . . Whitley and Ellis Young Senr. Justices (That were concerned in the sending of Thomas Rogers into Coll Bowles Regiment) and were kindly recd : but found before they came yt Thos. Rogers Brother was with them so desire that if he or his friends could agree wth ye officer to release him that they would not oppose it nor certifye agst the officer for soe doing wch they agreed to, and said they would doe nothing agst his discharge. And also signifyed they had nothing of a Peique agst him but were necessitated to raise men and soe sent him with five or 6 of his neighbours of the same town into ye Queens service etc.

Rd Diamond, Ed Wright with other Friends were appointed to draw up documents of sufferings etc. to present to Parliament for ease in ye case of tythes.

1715. The following signed Petition to Parliament for an alteration of affirmation.
        Gilbert Mollison
        Saml Arnold
        John Hopes
        John Haddon
        Lascelles Metcalfe
        John Freame.

These are all of them members of the London Lead Company.

Wright was a man of amazing energy, as we have evidence in the minutes of the Company that until close on his retirement in 1726 he was almost always the leader of the visiting deputation that travelled the whole country to examine mines and properties, travelling in this service almost every year to Wales, Derbyshire and the North, and on several occasions to Wanlock Head, Edinburgh, Stirling, and even the Orkneys and south-west Ireland. Throughout his connection with the Company, he was in control of all the smelting and refining processes, and his judgment was taken by the Court as final on all mines and mining problems. Along with Samuel Davis he originated and carried through the difficult negotiations by which the Ryton and Welsh Companies were amalgamated into the charter of the Governor and Company, and with Matthews he drew up and carried through the Company's financial policy. He is the only one of the early members to be commemorated in the literature of mining, his name being linked with the reverberatory furnace and the refining of silver by Schlüter, Percy, Farey and Wilson.

JOHN HADDON, born c. 1654.
Friends House Marriage and Burial Registers:
John Haddon of Southwark, Co. of Surrey, Smith, married Elizabeth Clarke at Horslydown 6.3.1676.

ELIZABETH HADDON died 16.4.1723 age 73 of Parish of St. Mary Magdalen Bermondsey, wife of John, buried at Long Lane, Bermondsey.

John Haddon died 13.3.1724 age 70 of Parish of St. George, Southwark, buried at Long Lane.

From Besse's *Sufferings of the Quakers*:
1687. Distresses in London. Taken also for the Trained-Bands by Warrants from the Lieutenancy.
John Haddon and other friends fined.

John Haddon lived first in Jacob Street, Southwark, then moved to Redriffe (Rotherhithe). The deed of one acre of ground for the first Haddonfield Meeting House in 1721 describes his residence as "By Cherry Garden on Thames Southwark, Blacksmith and Anchor Maker". (Cherry Garden Pier on the Thames lies east of Tower Bridge.) His name and that of his wife occur frequently in the minute books of Horslydown (Southwark Monthly Meeting). He helped to start the Meeting at Deptford about 1692 and was one of the trustees of the Meeting House there.

John Haddon was famous for being the father of a famous daughter, Elizabeth Estaugh (née Haddon). In 1701 she left England when about twenty-one (it is said under concern to make a home in America for travelling ministers), being entrusted by her father with large properties in West Jersey, America. It is not known why her father and mother did not leave England with her, though one suspects from the records of the Lead Company that he would find it difficult to get release from his varied connections in its business.

Elizabeth Haddon married a young Friend preacher in America, named John Estaugh, and the story of their courtship is told romantically by Longfellow in one of his Tales of a Wayside Inn, entitled " Elizabeth ". They built two houses during their married life, and perpetuated her maiden name in the name of one of their estates, which was called Haddonfield, and the present town of Haddonfield, New Jersey, gradually sprang up around the Estaugh homestead.

John and Elizabeth Estaugh had no children but adopted one of Elizabeth's nephews—Ebenezer Hopkins, and some of his descendants are alive in America to-day. A few items of Elizabeth Estaugh's furniture, along with letters and deeds, are still treasured in the hands of some of their descendants and at Haverford and Swarthmore Colleges.

John Haddon gave the ground for the first Friends' Meeting House at Haddonfield.

John Estaugh was agent for the Pennsylvania Land Company of London, and was succeeded by his nephew, Ebenezer Hopkins. The London Lead Company had some connection with this Land Company, but the relation is not very clear. The relative minutes appear in the Court minute books without any introduction or satisfactory ending, and are as follows : —

13th May 1707. Enoch Floyd, Ed. Wright, Peter Delannoy, S. Davis, Thos. Cooper, to consider motion re Land Co. and report their decision.

20th May 1707. Report of Floyd and others. Stock of Land Company is 60,000 acres of land in Pennsylvania, mostly already taken up and registered and Patents under the seal of the Province for the same and rest in good forwardness. They are to pay for same but two Beaver skins per annum if requested.

Clear of debts on this side and no debts in Pennsylvania.

Profit proposed to be made by land is by sale of it as may be thought fit. Thought by proprietors that the least the land will fetch will be £10 a 100 acres which is confirmed by some members of this Company who understand the value of land in Pennsylvania. If this Company can have a reasonable offer from the Land Company, it might be safe for this Company to procure the said land to be bought into the stock of this Company.

Pennsylvania Land Company proposed at the General Meeting 19th of May—to unite land shares with this Company at the rate of 4 land shares for one London Lead Company share.

Referred for further consideration.

17th August 1708. John Haddon moved that he thought it a proper time to discourse with the Pennsylvania Land Company again about the Proposal made by him (May 20th 1707) to bring the said land into this Corporation.

JOHN FREAME

A goldsmith of Lombard Street, and member of the Grocers' Company. Born 1668, died 1745.

In 1698, was a partner in the firm of bankers Freame & Gould, at the sign of the Three Anchors, Lombard Street, and was the banker for the Welsh Society of Mines Royal Copper. In 1728 he bought the freehold of No. 56 Lombard Street, the sign of the Black Spread Eagle, which remained the headquarters of his business, which later became Barclay's Bank, until 1770.

In 1697 he married Priscilla Gould, at Devonshire House, Bishopsgate, 19.vi.1697. He is mentioned in the registers as Citizen and Grocer, son of Robert Freame late of Cirencester in the county of Gloucester, clothier, deceased.

In 1711 John Freame was Clerk of Yearly Meeting.

In 1713 he published *Scripture Instruction* . . ., etc., the last edition of which was presented for the use of the Lancastrian Schools.

In 1733 his daughter Sally married James Barclay, the eldest son of David Barclay by his first wife Ann Taylor, and grandson of Barclay, author of the *Apology*. David Barclay's second wife was Priscilla Freame. The marriage connections were rather peculiar, and can be illustrated by two genealogical tables :—

BIOGRAPHICAL NOTES

FREAME.

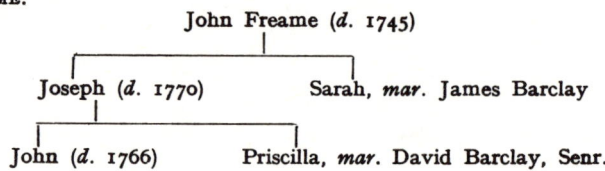

BARCLAY.

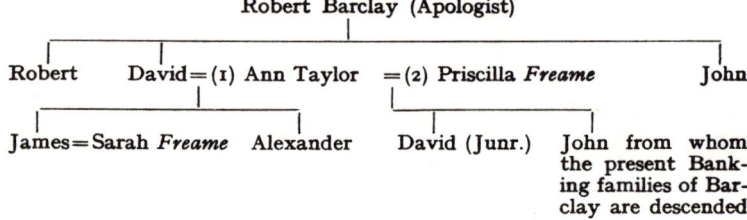

(Only the descendants connected with the Banking are mentioned.)

The son Joseph Freame succeeded his father John in the banking business of Freame & Gould, and took as partner in 1736 his brother-in-law, James Barclay, the firm becoming Freame & Barclay and afterwards, through various mutations, to Barclays Bank. A daughter of David Barclay Jun. married Richard Gurney of Norwich and so formed a link with other Quaker banking houses.

CHARLES ALSOPP

Was the first agent of the Company in the North, in 1704, and before that the agent and smelter for the Ryton Company from 1696.

6.xii.1703 married Lydia Brown of Broad Lee, at West Allendale Meeting, and on the taking of Whitfield Smelt Mill in 1706 he removed into Allendale to live. In 1716 he built his new home at Broadwood Hall, where the initials are still over the door, C. & L. A. 1716.

Charles Alsopp died 9.vi.1729, and Lydia his widow 23.x.1737.

There was a son and a large family of daughters, of whom :—

Lydia married Daniel Wren, 1723.
Hannah married Giles Raisby, 1725.

Sarah married John Graham of Sunderland, who wrote a very bitter pamphlet against Friends and was disowned.

Elizabeth married Thomas Bewley.

Rachel married Abraham Watson of Burnfoot, 10.v.1728. Watson was an active Friend in Alston Meeting, and a member of the family connected with Coanwood and later with Gateshead. The Watsons were closely linked with the Alsopps in the next generation through the granddaughters of Charles Alsopp.

```
                    Joshua Watson   = Ann Rutter
                    of Huntwell,
                    b. 1672, d. 1757

| | | | |
        Joshua Watson = Lydia d. Alsopp   Jacob      = Hannah d.
        of Riding,    of Broadwood,       b. 1748     Alsopp of
        b. 1746       m. 1769, d. 1810                Broadwood

                    Joseph = Rachel d. of Wm. Wigham
                             of Coanwood, m. 1782, d. 1794

| |
        William Watson = Elizabeth Richardson
                         of Coanwood

Esther = Joshua Watson of Newcastle,
         d. 1853 at Bensham, Gateshead
```

from whom are descended the Spence Watsons and Carrick Watsons, and with whom the Richardsons are connected.

Joseph Whitfield

Married Elizabeth Spark of Burnlaw, Allendale, in 1735. Was agent for the Company in Derbyshire from 1735 to 1776 when he returned to Allendale, to Burnlaw. Their son, Matthew Spark Whitfield, lived at Burnlaw but died in 1774, leaving two sons, the last of whom, Joseph, died in 1804 when the property passed to the grandfather of the present Friend owner, John Hall Shield.

Anthony Barker

Was agent for the Royal Mines Copper and the London Lead Company in Wales for many years, but beyond the mention of him in the minutes quoted in connection with Edward Wright, no details of him have been traced.

. . . .

BIOGRAPHICAL NOTES

Of the founders and prime movers of the Company, the above are all the scanty notes we have of the Friends, but there are short references to many of the people on the first lists of shareholders of the Ryton Company, the Royal Mines Copper, and the Lead Company, which are now quoted.

Share list of the Royal Mines Copper, Wales. April, 1702.

*Isaac Ashley	31	James Allen	5
*John Bellers	15	Sarah Bound	1
*John Bawne	15	William Chambers	4
*Thomas Cooper	50	*Richard Diamond	10
*Edward Dayley	4	*Thomas Davis	20
*John Freame	5	*Jacob Franklin	16
Enoch Floyd	13	*John Haddon	20
Urban Hall	22	Thomas Hart	5
William Hill	5	Richard Huffam	10
*John Heale	5	Thomas Kirkby	15
*John Knight	10	Peter Delannoy	40
Robert Long	5	William Monson	8
*Coxn Masen	20	John Matsen	20
Nathanial Matsen	20	Richard Matthews	100
*Lascelles Metcalfe		*Gibb Molleson	
*Roger Newham		Anne Moore	
*Matthew Plumstead		*Michael Russell	20
*Fra: Stamper	16	*James Tayler	15
William Thompson	30	John Tanner	5
*Edward Wright	23	*Abell Wilkinson	3
*Kathleen Wright	1		

MS. torn (bracketing Lascelles Metcalfe, Roger Newham, Matthew Plumstead)

Total of 645 shares.

List of people who transferred shares from the Ryton Company to the London Lead Company, in 1704.

*Mary Bawne	2	*Walter Benthall	2
John Clerke	1	*Richard Collett	2
*Thomas Cooper	2	*Edward Dayley	2
*John Haddon	4	*Joseph Heale	2
*William Kent	2	*John Knight	
Joseph Lacy		John Lambe	
*Thomas Lee	1	*John Pierrie	2
*Matthew Plumstead	1	*Nathaniel Rouse	
John Tanner	2	*Edward Wright	4

All those marked with an asterisk (*) took the form of affirmation in lieu of oath, and are assumed to be Friends.

LONDON LEAD COMPANY

Share list of the newly constituted London Lead Co. 1705.

*Isaac Ashley	21	*Patience Ashfield	10
*John Askew	5	Cahs. DuBois	20
*John Bellers	20	*Mary Bawne	20
James Brace	5	Sarah Bates	10
Christopher Croll	10	*Thomas Cooper	30
*Richard Collett	10	William Chambers	4
John Clerke	3	*Elizabeth Clay	10
*Thomas Davis	20	*Edward Dayley	25
*Richard Diamond	10	Enoch Floyd	13
*Jacob Ffranklin	16	*John Freame	5
Urban Hall	22	*John Haddon	20
*Joseph Heale	10	John Hester	30
*Thomas Hyam	4	Thomas Hale	5
*John Knight	10	*William Kent	8
Peter Delannoy	10	Edward Leeds	30
*Thomas Lee	2	Joseph Lacy	2
Richard Matthews	101	*Cornelius Mason	20
Matthew Matsen	40	*Lascelles Metcalfe	5
*Gilbert Molleson	5	*Mary Mason	10
*Rodger Newham	8	*Clement Plumstead	10
*John Pierrie	5	*Nathaniel Rous	5
*Mary Stamper	16	*James Taylor	15
John Tanner	10	*Edward Wright	36
*Abell Wilkinson	3	*Samuel Davis	50

Total shares 759.
£50 per share.

Friends House Registers provide the following :

JACOB FRANKLIN of Bishopsgate Street, Vintner, son of John Franklin of Whitechapel, married Mary Hinde on 11.9.1686 at Devonshire House.

CORNELIUS MASON of Cannon Street, Skinner, son of John Mason of Winchcomb in Gloucester, married Mary Bellers, daughter of Francis Bellers late of London at Bull and Mouth 1690.5.8.

THOMAS COOPER married Margery Smith at Bull and Mouth 1675.3.11.

JACOB FRANKLIN died 1710.2.30 age 49 of Peters Parish, Cornhill, Vintner died at his country house Bethleham Green, buried at Whitechapel.

CORNELIUS MASON died 1705.8.8 aged 48 of Swithins Parish London Stone, buried at Bunhill.

THOMAS COOPER died 1715.11.28 age 78 of Alie Street, Goodmans Fields Whitechapel, Citizen and Merchant Taylor, Leather dresser. Buried at Bunhill Fields.

EDWARD DAYLEY Died 18.1.1711 age 50. Linnen Draper of Parish of Mary Cheapside. Buried at Bunhill.

WILLIAM KENT Cheesemonger born 1650 son of Edward Kent of Oxfordshire died 1720.8.10 aged 70 of St. Botolph, Bishopsgate Without. Died at Bednal Green, buried at Bunhill.
Married (1) Anne Bathurst 1679.4.26.
(2) Margaret Cole in 1684.5.

JOHN ASKEW of Gracechurch Street Merchant son of Robert Askew of Lamesley in Bishoprick of Durham married Elizabeth Moore of Wapping at Ratcliff 29.11.1701/2.

CLEMENT PLUMSTEAD One of twelve proprietors of East New Jersey in 1682. Ironmonger at the Cross Sawers, nr Tower Hill in Minorys.

MICHAEL RUSSELL Had property in Suffolk and Middlesex and seems to have been of considerable means. George Fox stayed at his house. His daughter married Peter Collinson, the celebrated Botanist.

ISAAC ASHLEY, Merchant of Clement Danes Parish, son of Robert Ashley of Bragkirk, Cumberland, married Barbary Hutton at Bull and Mouth 1702. Died 9.11.1727 aged 74, late of Cannon Street, buried Bunhill Fields.

JAMES TAYLOR of Bishopsgate, Citizen and Loriner, died 1716.4.28.

ABEL WILKINSON living in Cheapside in 1682 at the death of a son (registers). Daughter married William Tooney. On the Quaker Workhouse Committee with Joseph Gee, sends in silk for spinning.

JOSEPH HEALE of Staines, Distiller, son of Richard Heale of Uxbridge, married Deborah Tanner at George Inn, Uxbridge, 1686.4.9. Died 7.8.1722 aged 59. Apothecary. A minister about thirty years. Buried at Uxbridge. Affectionate testimony from Monthly Meeting. Clerk of Yearly Meeting in 1712. Travelled in the ministry with Jonathan Gopsill, in Holland.

RICHARD DIAMOND, Mariner, son of Richard Diamond of Cornwall, married Margaret Gilbert of Bermondsey at Horslydown in 1681.11.12—became a Merchant. Before that made many voyages to America. Died 10.7.1732 aged 84 in Parish of Camberwell. Buried Long Lane, Bermondsey. On Workhouse Committee.

LASCELLES METCALFE, Citizen and Merchant Taylor, son of Robert Metcalfe late of Sowerby, Parish of Sexton, Co. York. Married at Devonshire House, 1691, Christian, daughter of Thomas Cox, a wealthy Vintner. On London Workhouse Committee. Original Sufferings at Friends House, p. 258, state he had goods taken including " 31 yards of tick, etc.".

GILBERT MOLLISON ? of Aberdeen, brother-in-law of Robert Barclay. Prominent member of Peel (London) Monthly Meeting. On Workhouse Committee.

THOMAS LEE of Old Street, London, tailor, son of Michael Lee of Hendley, Salop, married Grace Burt of London, 26.1.1702. Died aged 30 on 27.5.1709.

ROGER NEWHAM, On Workhouse Committee in 1702, of Wapping Stepney, mariner, son of R.N. of Staley in Derbyshire, married Thomasin Buchsher at Ratcliffe 13.2.1703.

WALTER BENTHALL, late of the Island of Barbadoes, Merchant, married Mercy Eccleston, daughter of Rich. E. decd. and Priscilla now wife of Thos. Hart of Enfield, at Devonshire House on 6.1.1683. Died 7.6.1709, late of Lombard Street. Buried Bunhill, aged 65.

PATIENCE ASHFIELD, 1627-1704, widow of Richard Ashfield. Friends at Staines met in her house before their first Meeting House was built. Wrote an account of the life and death of her husband.

RICHARD COLLETT of Charing Cross, Westminster, Vintner, married Elizabeth Hern 16.12.1687, later of Dartford, Kent.

In 1695 back in Spittle Square, London.

In 1696 of Threadneedle Street, London.

Died 27.6.1721 aged 65 at Stamford Hill, buried at Bunhill.

JOHN KNIGHT, died 1740.6.27 aged 85, buried at Bunhill.

MARY BAWNE, 1720.2.23 died aged 71 late of London. Widow of John Bawne, Brewer. Buried at the Park, Southwark.

JOHN BELLERS, 1654-1725, Son of Francis Bellers, Grocer, of London. John B. was a Cloth Merchant and early began philanthropic work (see *John Bellers* by A. R. Fry, 1935).

JOHN PEIRIE of Houndsditch, Citizen and Draper, son of James P., late of Turrolfe, Aberdeenshire. Married Mary Mackell at Devonshire House 29.12.1703/4. Died 7.12.1718 aged 67. Buried at Bunhill.

THE STAGG FAMILY

JOSHUA STAGG started with the Company as a miner in Teesdale in 1775, later promoted to be a mine agent in Upper Teesdale. In 1813 made mine agent for Teesdale at a salary of £140 per annum.

In 1816 promoted to district agent for all Teesdale at salary of £200, increased at various subsequent times. Died April 1824, making forty-eight years continuous service. He did much to introduce the idea of " overmen " into the mines, a suggestion later carried to completion by his nephew.

JOSHUA STAGG, Junior. Son of the above Joshua Stagg, was appointed to be mill agent at Egglestone, and to assist his father at Middleton, in 1816. Was making good progress with the improvement of smelting methods, but was taken ill and died in the Company's service, 1824.

JOSHUA C. STAGG, son of the above Joshua Jun., appointed to be clerk to the Company at Marton, Westmorland, in 1824, at salary of £50. In 1831 salary increased to £100 and good reports given of him, but in 1832 he resigned and left the district.

This succession of Staggs, father, son and grandson, was almost entirely connected with the mining side of the Company, and their chief contributions are technical. The brother of the first Joshua Stagg was Robert Stagg, and his two sons, Joseph and Robert, did much to carry out the great social programme of the Company that we have been considering in detail; it will, therefore, be of interest to follow their careers in greater detail than some of the others, and fortunately there is more material available, though mainly in the form of sparse minutes and letter endorsements in the letter book index.

ROBERT STAGG was in the employ of the Company as a miner, at the same time as his brother Joshua, i.e. in 1775, and in 1778 was appointed a mining agent, to reside at

Middleton-in-Teesdale, " having been recommended to the notice of the Deputation in that year as an able and good miner, by Robert Percival, the Company's then principal agent ". Robert Stagg was promoted in 1796 to the office of " Cashier and Superintendent of all the Company's smelting works, of washing the ore, of the ore carriage, and of forwarding the Company's Lead from the Mills to Bladon and Stockton ". This was a new post, created for him to occupy, and largely grew out of the suggestions he and his brother made from time to time for better co-ordination of the various processes of mining. To quote one brief minute, fortunately preserved among the mining records of the Company, " the first lesson he taught his children, was in his own quaint and brief way—' Whensoever any doubt may arise between your Purse and your Conscience be sure and let your Purse pay, but keep your Conscience clear ' ; a maxim which he enforced and exemplified in his own conduct, and in the departments under his control and that of his son Joseph, not one single indirect or questionable matter was found." This was indeed the keynote to all his improvements in the Company's organization, he worked hard to maintain perfectly frank and friendly contact between all persons employed by the Company, whether washer boys or members of the Court. He died on 7.6.1808 and was succeeded by his son Joseph.

JOSEPH STAGG received the same appointment from the Court as his father had enjoyed. At the time of his appointment, 18.8.1808, he was thirty-four years of age, having been brought up under his father, in the Company's employment, from the age of sixteen. In consequence of ill health he applied to the Court, in 1809, to be allowed the assistance of his brother Robert, to which application the Court made answer, 30.3.1809, " You are to inform the Court whether your brother be free from all engagements, in which case it is the Court's intention to meet your wishes by appointing him (for the present) agent at Stanhope Mill, upon the principle that he be instructed by you, till he shall gain a competent knowledge to fill the situation—he is also to assist you as above mentioned and to prepare (under your directions) all documents necessary for the Company's accounts." Joseph Stagg died 19.11.1809 and his brother was transferred from Stanhope to fill his place at Middleton-in-Teesdale.

Apart from the numerous entries in the minutes relating to Robert Stagg, there is among the documents still preserved a short memoir of him, and from the two sources a fairly complete account can be given. The first part will be taken from the minutes, and will in consequence be more brief.

ROBERT STAGG, born at Middleton-in-Teesdale 30.9.1781, and entered the employment of the Company as a boy, working variously on the washing floors, in the smelt mills, and later in the offices, but after some time being employed by some other mining concern in the district, possibly at the Duke of Cleveland's smelt mill.

1809.13.4. Appointed to Stanhope Mill, and as assistant to his brother in the accounting department at Middleton.

1810.24.5. Appointed to succeed his brother as cashier and superintendent of smelting, etc., at a salary of £500 a year.

In 1813 he was able to report considerable improvements made in the mill department, amongst others, his greatest work being the completion of experiments started by his uncle and brother on the effect of roasting ores before smelting. " By a recent trial made, Matthew Johnson (the smelter) reports that the same quantity of ore and of the same quality, producing only 57 pieces of Lead without roasting, produced 66 pieces after that process." The savings effected in wages by improved methods of working are £3,376 per annum. He requested on presentation of this report that he be allowed to visit and inspect different smelting works, to study a variety of methods, and this was readily agreed to. This early interest in smelting became confirmed, and some of the greatest technical advances in lead smelting and refining were made under his management of the mills. By 1818 he was able to report on this department, " I believe I may be allowed to say that in the Mill results, we now stand alone in this part of the country ; and may safely challenge a comparison with any of our neighbours as well on the score of produce as on that of economy." In 1813 the Court " Resolved that he be desired to accept the sum of £500 as a mark of the Court's high approbation of his service."

In 1816 he was appointed general superintendent of all districts. About this time there are occasional reports to the Court that he is suffering from a return of the complaint in the breast, with a cough, etc., and after a few weeks from the works to recuperate, he was feeling so bad as to ask leave to resign his appointment. The Court presented a watch, with inscription, to him, but soon after learn that his improvement is such that he will continue for a little longer before resigning. He reports great difficulties in his visits to Alston Moor, because of snow-drifted tracks and lack of good roads, and begins to plan his great road reform that has already been detailed. The Court instructed him always to have an attendant on such journeys and when visiting mines.

In the winter of 1816 he took up with the Court the question of the dearness of food in the northern districts, and evolved the food distribution schemes already detailed in an earlier chapter. In December of 1816 he was ordered South for three or four months for treatment of his chest complaint, and proposed to the Court to avail himself of that opportunity to visit the mines of Cornwall and Derbyshire. This was done with great benefit to his health, and the addition of much wider experience of mining problems from those fields. In 1817 he proposed that the Company's principle of always having some exploration trials on hand should be systematized at a definite proportion of the workmen and capital employed, and urged that the trials should be used to secure a succession of good mines, promising trials being substituted for old and dangerous mines from time to time. His salary was increased that year to £1,000 and an annuity of £300 granted for fourteen years certain, to accumulate for the benefit of his family, " considering his intense application, the extraordinary difficulties he has had to encounter, and what his unremitting exertions have accomplished, at the sacrifice of his health and comfort ".

After many serious setbacks in health, and worry over an increasing swelling in the side, he is able to report that his complaint has been treated differently and he is enjoying much better health. In spite of this it is reported again in 1818 that his lungs are very delicate, and throughout his life illnesses, mainly chest and lung trouble, but occasional fevers, are recurrent ; it is the more remarkable that with this very severe handicap he carried out such widespread and varied schemes for the well-being of the communities under his care.

After 1820 he made a practice of residing the winter at one of the Westmorland centres of the Company, either Marton or Dufton, and this made his winters much more endurable.

In 1824 the Court order his portrait to be painted by Ramsey and hung in the Court room, London, 19 Martins Lane, Cannon Street. Between 1818 and 1826 he undertook the redesign of the smelt mills at Nent Head and Eggleston, with astonishing results in the way of increased efficiency and improved quality of lead, and also with considerable saving on costs. His savings in the organization of the works were returned to him for use in the social schemes he so much loved, and it is perhaps most enlightening of all that remains in the way of records to see how constantly he appeals to the Court for permission to make some improvement in conditions, and the Court respond with unlimited encouragement and enthusiasm, and grant all the sums asked for without question. They gave him all the encouragement that was humanly possible, and gained a rich reward in his unswerving loyalty and his growing skill as organizer and smelter. It was indeed a happy relationship throughout his life, and typical of the general relation between the Court and its agents for more than two centuries. In 1827 a piece of plate, value £150, was voted to him, " in approbation, etc., especially as regards the workings in Alston Moor, also a gold case for the Watch presented in 1816 ".

In 1835 the Court gave him leave of absence to visit the mines of Derbyshire and Wales, taking his son with him, as part of the boy's training for employment by the Company.

In 1836 his son, aged twenty-four, was appointed as his assistant, but he insisted that the salary paid his son should be deducted from his own. From that winter until 1842 he had more frequent attacks of illness, and in 1839 was compelled by the Company's medical officer to remove into Yorkshire, to live at Dishforth, for the sake of his health. He tendered his resignation to the Court, who were eventually satisfied that his system of mine and smelting organization was thoroughly sound, and capable of persisting even without Stagg's personality behind it, so in consideration of his need of a rest they regretfully accepted it, and finally relieved him of all duties in 1842. A timepiece and a Bible were presented to him in 1843, with the following inscription.

Plate XVI   The Enginers' shop yard, Middleton in Teesdale.

Plate XVII   London Lead Company, Smelthouse yard at Blackton Mill, Eggleston, Teesdale. (Beamish Museum).

Plate XVIII Entrance to Haggs Level, Nentsberry Mine. (Beamish Museum).

Plate XIX The Smelt Mill and Brewery Shaft with the water blast headgear. Nent Head Village in the distance.

Plate XX   Nent Head. Procession at the coronation of King Edward VII, 1902.

Plate XXI   Middleton Hall, headquarters of the London Lead Company, designed and built by Bonomi in 1819. (Beamish Museum).

Plate XXII Pattinson Pans in the Smelt Mill, used for the recovery of silver from the lead.

Plate XXIII Water wheel at Coldberry Mine, Teesdale. There are noggs for three stamps and gear wheel for a set of crushing rollers. (Beamish Museum).

January 1843

Presented to Robert Stagg esq. on his retirement from the Superintendence of the Lead Company's Concerns in the North of England, by the Company's Agents, Clerks, Overmen, and Workmen ; as a token of their affectionate regard and esteem, and of their grateful remembrance of his numerous and successful efforts for the promotion of the best interests of every party engaged in the Company's service.

After much correspondence he was persuaded to retain the duties of cashier, and £500 a year was paid to him for that work until 1851, when he relinquished his last post with them.

In 1861 a " testimonial to Robert Stagg " was ordered to be placed in each of the Company's new schools, and a copy of the one at Alston has been given in Chapter I.

He died in retirement at Dishforth, 27.3.1864.

JOSEPH D. STAGG, son of Robert, born in 1815, was appointed under his father to Egglestone Mill in 1832, to act as overman at the mill and to study smelting. In 1835 he was reported as a young man of great promise, and sent with his father to study mines in Cornwall and Derbyshire, and also given special help to study chemistry and metallurgy under some of the Durham University staff. He was removed to Middleton to study the office organization, again under his father, and in 1836 his salary was increased to £300 a year to act as assistant to his father in any department he needed special help. He was married in that year.

In 1839 he was appointed deputy superintendent, associated, on account of his youth, with R. W. Bainbridge.

His father's great interest in lead smelting was transferred by the son to the refining of silver, and from 1840 to 1850 he made many improvements in the new Pattinson process of silver extraction, and also in furnace design.

In 1842 he was appointed manager of the mills, washing floors and counting house, thus taking over his father's duties. He seems to have inherited much of his father's ill health, and after several severe illnesses tendered his resignation to the Court in 1844. This was accepted, and a gratuity of £200 given him for his services in the refining department.

He died in Scotland in 1851, from inflammation of the lungs.

ROBERT WALTON BAINBRIDGE, son of Robert Bainbridge, the Company's solicitor, became the next superintendent of the concern after the Stagg family, and his family remained in high position with the Company until the very last years.

Robert Walton Bainbridge was born in 1804, and educated as a barrister, assisting his father on the Company's business.

In 1839 he was associated with Joseph Stagg on his (J.S.) appointment as deputy superintendent, and was put into the various departments of the works to train as a possible successor to Joseph Stagg in case of need, at the same time remaining the Company's legal adviser in succession to his father.

In 1840 he was appointed general mine agent, and in 1841 chief mine agent for the whole area. In 1842 he was formally appointed successor to Joseph Stagg as superintendent of the whole concern. The following year the deputation make good reports of his efficiency, but note that he is in a somewhat difficult position with his brother-in-law, but although this matter is not made clear in the minutes, there is a later note that the trouble has been cleared up. His period of office, until 1868, was marked by steady continuance of the previous policy, and is not marked by any alteration of either processes or organization. He continued in every way the concern exactly as the Staggs left it, and was able to bring it successfully through many trying periods. His principal contribution was naturally made on the legal aspects of the Company's relationship to the various Lords of the Manor, and before his period of service was finished he secured some rationalization of the multiple leases they held, and also obtained a simpler and reduced reckoning of the royalty or " duty " ore paid to the lessors.

ROBERT BAINBRIDGE, father of Robert Walton, just discussed, acted as manager of the Company's estates from 1810 to 1853 and as the Company's solicitor. He was succeeded by his son.

UTRICK BAINBRIDGE, brother of the superintendent, who served as land agent and solicitor in the North from 1853 till some time after 1865.

Two sons of Robert Walton Bainbridge, ROBERT and HENRY GEORGE, were taken into the Company. Robert was placed in the counting house in 1856, but in spite of very promising reports left the Company in 1857 to become a farmer.

HENRY GEORGE BAINBRIDGE entered the counting house in 1858, in his seventeenth year, and was promoted rapidly in that department until 1866, when he was made manager of the mills, washing floors, and the Company's houses. He remained in the Company's employ until after 1869.

GOVERNORS OF THE GOVERNOR AND COMPANY FOR SMELTING DOWN LEAD WITH PIT COAL AND SEA COAL

1692-1704	Richard Owen
1704-1707	Samuel Davies
1707-1729	Urban Hall
1729-1731	Enoch Floyd
1731-1733	Charles du Bois
1733-1742	John Freame
1742-1753	Cornelius Mason
1753-1762	Thomas Hyam
1762-1782	James Mathias
1782-1795	Jacob Hagen
1795-1811	Thomas Cooper
1811-1817	Jacob Hagen
1817-1823	James Palmer
1823-1824	Thomas How Masterman
1824-1840	John Hillersdon
1840-1860	John Masterman
1860-1869	Octavius Wigram
1869-1884	John William Birch
1884	William Knox Wigram
1884-1900	Frederick Halsey Janson
1900-1905	John Foskett

INDEX

accidents, 57, 58
ALSOPP, Charles, 78, 152, 28, 29, 31
Alston Moor, 12, 13, 104, 138, 140
Alva mine, Stirling, 124
Anglezark, Lancashire, 119
annuities, 51
assay laboratories, 69

BAINBRIDGE, Henry G., 164, 165
BAINBRIDGE, Robert junr, 164
BAINBRIDGE, Robert W., 164
BAINBRIDGE, Utrick, 164
bands, 71
BARCLAY, pedigree, 152
BARKER, Anthony, 104, 113, 134, 137, 153
baths, public, 23
Bawtry, traffic to, 84, 85
blast engine, 144, 145
BRINDLEY, James, 84, 85, 86
Bristol Company, 96, 129
buddles, 142

calcining ores, 69
canals, 84-7
capital, 123, 126, 127, 130
carriage, 88, 89, 90, 91
chapels, 20, 25
chemical lectures, 69
Cherry Tree Hill Estate, 19
CLERK, Talbot, 99, 129
Coanwood, 81
coinage, 111, 112
COOPER, Thomas, 100, 103, 154, 155, 156
copper mines, 96, 103, 129
corn, purchase of, 31-8
Court of Assistants, 11, 98, 99, 127, 130
CROWLEY, Ambrose, 78, 79

DAVIES, Samuel, 100, 105, 113, 155, 165
Dee, river navigation, 117
Deputation reports, 27
Derbyshire, 83, 84, 85, 119, 120, 123, 137, 140
Derwent mines, 8, 75, 81, 131
dressing floors, 21, 23, 139, 143
Dufton estate, 25, 27, 50, 58, 71

education, 56
Egglestone, 14, 58, 71, 111, 131
epidemics, 50, 53, 54
ESTAUGH, John and Elizabeth, 149

food supplies, 30, 31, 42, 43
FORSTER, Arnold, F., 65
FREAME, John, 151, 152, 154, 155, 165
Friendly Mining Society, 82
Friendly Societies, 45

Gadlis, N.Wales, 77, 78, 104, 108, 116, 117, 118, 131, 134, 137
gardens, 20, 27, 28
Garrigill, 24, 25, 27, 28, 31, 50, 71
General Court Minutes, 10
Governor and Company, 97, 98, 99, 105, 106, 107
GRAVES, George, 119
GREENHOW, Dr, 50
Greenwich Hospital, 10, 12, 138, 141
gunpowder, 139

Hackett Forge, Langdale, 103
HADDON, John, 103, 105, 113, 149, 154, 155
Haddon Land Company, Pennsylvania, 150, 151
Hilton Estate, 25, 27
horses in the mines, 92
Horticultural Societies, 20, 27

Ireland, 118, 119
Isle of Man, 123

JAMES, Mr, schoolmaster, 63, 64
JOHNSTON, Professor J. F. W., 69

Lake District, 96, 103, 129, 130
libraries, 71
London Lead Company, 12, 13, 17, 27, 94, 97, 107-111, 130, 139, 148, 155
Long Marton, 71
LOUIS, Dr Henry, 9
Lunehead, Yorkshire, 14

MACADAM, J. L., 90
MASON, Cornelius, 155

170

INDEX   171

Medical Officer, 46-9
MENNELL, Henry T., 9
MENNELL, George H., 9
Middleton-in-Teesdale, 14, 25, 26, 27, 29, 57, 71
Mill Close Mine, Derbyshire, 123, 138
mine overmen, 72, 73
mine shops, 15, 16
Mining Council, 74
minute books, 10, 15

Nent Head, 13, 14, 17-23, 28, 39, 130, 131
NEWTON, Sir Isaac, 111, 112, 113
Northern area, 14

ore dressing, 21, 22, 141, 142
ore hearth, 138, 139, 140
Orkneys, 81, 82, 123
OWEN, Robert, 57

pack horses, 79, 80, 83, 88
pasture improvement, 28
plans, 55
plantations, 28, 29, 30
Pennsylvania Land Company, 150, 151
Priorsdale Estate, 13, 24, 25, 28, 29, 30
profits, 127, 131, 167

Quaker affirmations, 105, 106
Quaker industrialists, 95
Quaker Lead Company, 11, 12, 107, 146, 147
'Quaker shillings', 112
Quakers, 146-158

railways, 92, 93
Rampgill washing floor, 21, 22, 141
reading rooms, 71
Ready Money Shop, 20, 38
reverberatory furnace, 120, 129, 132, 134, 138, 140
roads, 14, 25, 79, 83, 87, 88, 89
Royal Charters, 97, 128, 129, 130
Royal Mines Copper, 10, 100, 103, 106, 108, 147, 154
Ryton Company, 10, 103, 108, 134, 138
Ryton on Tyne, 77, 78, 81, 104, 108, 139

schools, 57-66
SHIELD, James Hall, 9
silver, 76, 108, 109, 110, 111, 112, 113
smelting, 80, 96, 120, 129

smelt mills:
  Acton, 81, 131, 132
  Blagill, 138
  Bollihope, 14, 111
  Bowers, 83, 120, 121, 123, 137, 138
  Bristol, 99, 100, 129
  Dufton, 25
  Egglestone, 14, 111, 131
  Gadlis, 77, 78, 104, 108, 116, 117, 118, 134, 137
  Jeffries, 131
  Kilboy, Ireland, 119
  Nent Head, 19, 131, 132, 133, 138
  Ryton, 78, 81, 104, 108
  Stanhope, 14, 132
  Tynehead, 79, 104
  Wanlock Head, 82
  Whitfield, 80, 81, 131
social policy, 94
Society of Miners, 40-6
soughs, 138
STAGG, Joshua, 158
STAGG, Joseph, 57, 159
STAGG, Joshua junr, 158
STAGG, Joshua C., 158
STAGG, Joseph D., 163
STAGG, Robert, 22, 160
stamps, 139
Stanhope, 57, 63, 71, 132
steam engine, 118
Sunday Schools, 57, 60

table separator, 142
Teesdale, 13, 14, 30, 89, 122, 140, 143
Tynebottom Mill, Garrigill, 31
Tynehead, 71, 79, 104

VERNATTY, Constantine, 97
Vielle Montagne Zinc Company, 10, 13

Wages, 18, 32, 128
Wales, 39, 77, 78, 104, 108, 116, 118, 140
Wanlock Head, Scotland, 82
wash house and baths, 23
water balance, 143
water blast, 143, 144
water supply to villages, 50
WATSON, pedigree, 153
Weardale, 122, 140
weather records, 15
welfare, 134, 140, 141
Wensleydale, 125
Wensley, Derbyshire, 120, 137

Westmorland estates, 14, 25, 71
WHITFIELD, Joseph, 84, 137, 153
Winster, Derbyshire, 120
Workmen's Fund, 46, 50
WRIGHT, Dr Edward, 95, 100, 103, 108, 113, 114, 125, 130, 134, 146-9, 154, 155

Yorkshire, 14, 71, 75, 125, 140

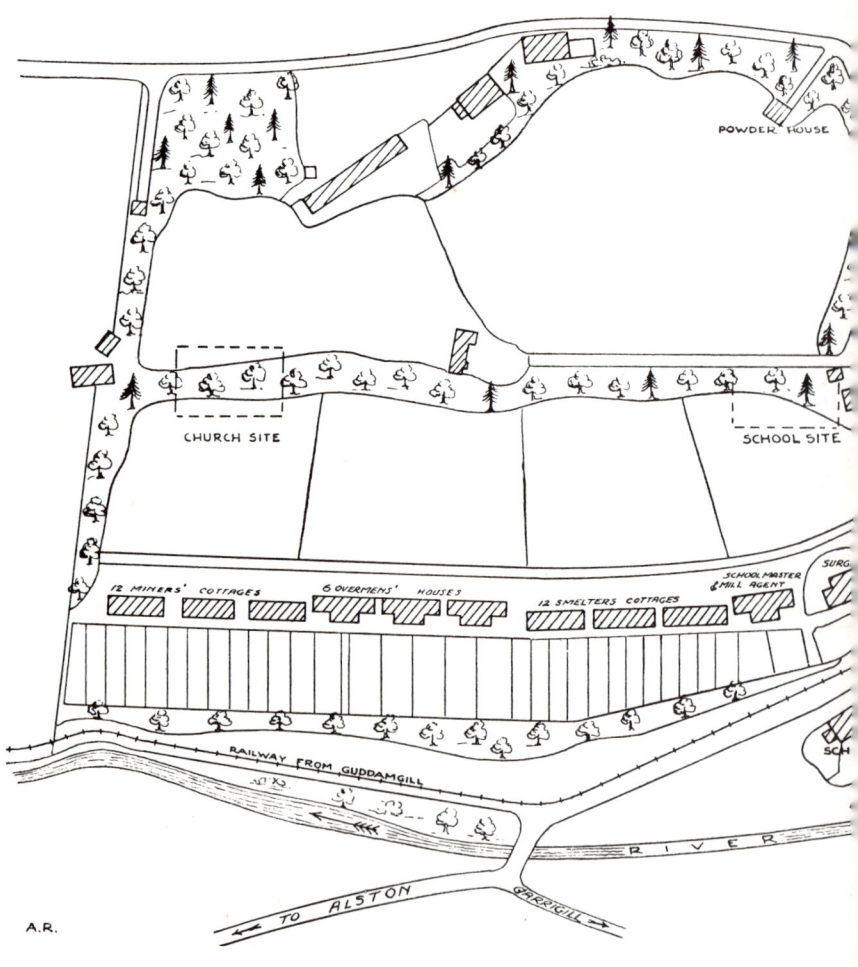